HIDDEN IN MY HEART

WILMA DAFFERN

©TXu000688793 / 1995-04-11

ISBN: 978-0-578-04391-3

Wilma Daffern
P. O. Box 595
Fountain, CO 80817
Phone: (719) 683-4289
Email: daffern@elpasotel.net
www.hiddeninmyheart.info

DEDICATION

This book is dedicated to my family.

ACKNOWLEDGMENTS

Rev. Anthony Simowitz, the pastor under whom I found Christ.

Joyce Rose, a Christian lady who introduced me to Child Evangelism Fellowship.

Pastor Bob McGuire, the pastor who went through Carrie's illness with us.

Carrie's Christian doctor in Bartlesville.

All of those who have prayed for, or ministered to my family and me.

To all of you my sincere thanks!

HIDDEN IN MY HEART

Love is a flag flown high from the castle in my heart
From the castle in my heart
From the castle in my heart
Love is a flag flown high from the castle in my heart
When the King is in residence here.

Peace is a flag flown high from the castle in my heart
From the castle in my heart
From the castle in my heart
Peace is a flag flown high from the castle in my heart
When the King is in residence here.

Joy is a flag flown high from the castle in my heart
From the castle in my heart
From the castle in my heart
Joy is a flag flown high from the castle in my heart
When the King is in residence here.

CHORUS
So lift it high in the sky let the whole world know
Let the whole world know;
Let the whole world know
So lift it high in the sky let the whole world know
That the King is in residence here.

(copied)

The lyrics on the previous page describe how I feel today with joy so full I must fly it high in the sky and let the whole world know. I'm sitting in a hospital room by the bedside of my fifteen-year-old daughter, Carrie. She is in a coma. Songs at midnight? Isn't that what God promises His children? How dark the night would be without Jesus; how hopeless this situation.

Carrie has had many physical problems. She has lived many times when the doctors said it was almost impossible, only to have one say, "We've kept her body alive with the use of machines, but she'll never be any more than a mummy. She'll never come off the machines. She'll never move again. Her mind is gone. There is no hope."

"But I will hope continually and will yet praise thee more and more" (Psalm 71:14).

CHAPTER 1

DEFYING ALL ODDS!

". . . for whatever is not of faith is sin" (Romans 14:23; KJV).

Carrie had almost finished her freshman year of high school when she arrived home one evening exhausted from another victorious track meet. She showed us her ribbons, then ate dinner and went to bed. This caused me to be very concerned because she is diabetic. After encouraging Carrie to check her glucose level three times, she became a bit frustrated and assured me that she was fine, simply tired. She fussed, "Look at Rockie. She's tired too." And she was right, Rockie, our second daughter, had come home from the same track meet, eaten, and fallen to sleep as well. So I let Carrie go to sleep also. I checked her several times during the night, and as far as I could tell she was just asleep.

We don't know whether a difficulty arose with her diabetes from the track meet that day, if a bad case of flu she had suffered earlier physically upset her more than realized, or if perhaps another unknown problem developed, but what had seemed to be controllable health problems had grown severe and out of control. Carrie had not just gone to sleep; she had slipped into a coma. The next morning I couldn't wake her up.

Carrie was taken to the hospital in Independence, Kansas, on May 1, 1975. During the night she became critical and the following day was moved by ambulance to a larger hospital in Bartlesville, Oklahoma. Upon her arrival in Bartlesville, Carrie was placed in a semi-private room on the first floor. It wasn't a coincidence that the doctor said that room was not large enough to work with her and had her moved to a hospital room next to the coronary care unit. We were later told this probably saved her life in the crisis to follow. Looking back now, I have no doubt that all of her physical hardships were allowed under the watchful eye of the Lord. It is evident that God went before us all the way.

The following weeks were filled with crisis after crisis. It is impossible to explain all the physical trauma Carrie suffered in detail, and to even try would take a doctor and no doubt fill many pages. However, so as to give a little understanding of the scope of God's miracles throughout Carrie's illness, I will list a few of the complications Carrie experienced. I will also write about some of these details individually in later pages, bringing out what God taught me through them.

Carrie did need a miracle! After entering the coma, she suffered three heart arrests, pneumonia twice, severe internal bleeding, surgery to remove much of her stomach, and then her body quit producing protein, causing her to swell very badly. She also suffered from phlebitis, several infections, and had an elevated temperature much of the time- once it ran from 104 to 106 degrees for almost three weeks. She suffered from convulsions and her blood glucose went as high as 800 and as low as 0. When her glucose level dropped to 0, it caused additional breathing problems.

Carrie was placed on a respirator after her first heart arrest, which gave her a little help breathing, but it also added another danger. Carrie's body could possibly learn to rely on a respirator, which meant that she might be unable to breathe on her own again. An endotracheal tube was inserted in her throat to help keep her airway open. In addition to these numerous physical problems, she had many injections, tests, and etc. Carrie set a record for this hospital, in the first three weeks, for the number of tests run in a certain area.

Through all of this, we have seen God's power in action! According to the doctors, it was almost impossible for her to have lived through these complications. It reached the place where my husband, Charles, and I felt almost honored to have been chosen to witness such power. Surely Carrie's testimony could be, "According to my earnest expectation and my hope, that in nothing shall I be ashamed, but that with all boldness, as always, so now also Christ shall be magnified in my body, whether it be by life or by death. For to me to live is Christ, and to die is gain" (Philippians 1:20-21 KJV).

As for the rest of my family and me, although there were many rough times, mostly we felt only peace. We felt very weak and tired, but still had that deep peace that only God can give. It was the peace that is described in Philippians 4:7 KJV, so we knew God was in charge and all would be well. "And the peace of God, which passeth all understanding, shall keep your hearts and minds through Christ Jesus."

We were told that prayer requests for Carrie and our family were going up in many cities, with many people praying. In fact, they stopped in the middle of a secular radio program in our hometown and had special prayer, even though we had moved away ten years earlier when Carrie was only five years old. How God upheld us in prayer is more miraculous than I can imagine, and I'm sure I won't know the full scope of this until I reach Heaven.

But still, at times we took over, for God had much to

teach us through this situation. Oh, I knew most of it before because I had memorized and taught many of the verses He used, however, when you live them in a crisis of this scope they become heart knowledge, which is far more than just head knowledge. In Romans 5:4 the word used is "experience."

Our pastor heard about Carrie and immediately came to the Bartlesville hospital. Praise the Lord for concerned pastors! He sat with us many long hours, both reading the scriptures and praying; and of course, we prayed also. Somehow, though, it seemed like we were so tired and so closely involved that I didn't have the strength to really seek out God's will and pray accordingly as I usually did. My prayer was more of a heartfelt, "Lord, this is in your hands. Thy will be done." Later, I did ask Him to show us His will so I could pray accordingly. As her mother, I had a deep hope in my heart that the Lord would heal Carrie and give her back to us, but even more than this I wanted His will to be done, for Him to be glorified and people to be won to Christ through this hardship.

The scripture God laid on our pastor's heart was Mark 5:22-43-the story of Jairus and his twelve-year-old daughter whom Jesus healed. Believing this was what God wanted for Carrie, we prayed for healing.

It's awesome how God would always prepare us ahead of time for each crisis that arose. One day I received a phone call from a friend. She commented, "I don't know why I called. I simply felt I had to tell you we are praying for Carrie and you." I thanked her and walked back to Carrie's room. By now her heart had stopped for the second time, but she appeared to be stabilized. As I approached the room, the doctor came out and said that her heart had stopped a third time, but was again started and perhaps even more stable than before. I know that my friend's telephone call was to prepare us for this heart arrest. Even so, I found her heart stopping three times too many. Charles and his sister walked up the hall, I began to weep. "How many times," I cried, "How many times can she go through this?"

Our pastor instantly began to pray, and as he prayed, I wept. After a few minutes had passed, I quit crying and he quit praying-at least out loud-and we sat in silence. Then he asked, "What are your thoughts at this point?" I grinned and replied, "I can only think of one thing. A verse keeps running through my mind, 'Whatever is not of faith is sin.'"

CHAPTER 2

I CAN'T CARRY IT

"My grace is sufficient" (2 Corinthians 12:9 KJV).

After Carrie's third heart arrest, her condition remained stabilized for about two days. By now I had become extremely exhausted. Several days had passed since the beginning of this illness, and considering her stabilized condition, I decided to go home and get a good night's sleep. That evening I realized just how difficult it was going to be if we lost Carrie. I needed a notebook that I had left in her bedroom, but I found I couldn't make myself walk into the room to pick it up. Thinking she might not return to this room was just too much for me to handle.

As I stood unable to enter her room, I thought back to the time when we were waiting while the doctors worked on her after her first heart arrest. An incident in Corrie Ten Boom's book, *The Hiding Place*, came to mind. Corrie tells of the time when she was ten or eleven years old and riding a train with her father. She had heard a word she didn't understand and asked her father what it meant. In his fatherly wisdom, he set his heavy travel case filled with watches and parts down on the floor, and then asked her to carry it off the train for him. When she tried to lift it she protested, "It's too heavy." "Yes," he replied, "and it would be a pretty poor father who would ask his little girl to carry such a load." He continued to explain that this was the way it was with knowledge. Some was too heavy for children, but when she was older and stronger she would be able to bear it. He finished by adding that for now, "You must trust me to carry it for you." Corrie was satisfied with his answer. In later years, when she was in the Nazi prison camp and circumstances seemed unbearable, she would say to her Heavenly Father, "This is too heavy; I can't carry it; You carry it for me."

When I read her book, I was so impressed with the wisdom Father Ten Boom possessed in dealing with his children that I stopped and asked God to give me this same kind of wisdom when dealing with my own. Looking back, as we waited while the doctors worked on Carrie, all of this took on a different meaning. I prayed and asked God to carry this. As I stood by her bedroom door unable to make myself go in, I remembered praying and asking God to carry this ordeal and again I prayed, "Heavenly Father, if you're going to take her, it's going to be too heavy for me. I won't be able to carry it. You carry it for me. I believe you've promised you'll carry this; that You will give us as much grace as we need to get us through. I ask You for this grace and I receive it. Thank You. In Jesus' name I pray. Amen."

Lifting my head high, I walked into Carrie's bedroom, looked around and started remembering things about Carrie. For fifteen years, Charles and I had watched our oldest daughter grow and blossom into a young lady. Carrie has beautiful red hair and sky blue eyes. She loves the outdoors. Carrie is an excellent athlete often winning in whatever sport she participates in. Seeing her first place ribbons for shot-put and relays were a regular occurrence. Carrie loves animals, especially horses.

Carrie also loves her family. She refers to her little brother, David, as her "buddy" often carrying him on her shoulders and taking him for walks. I am not one of those mothers who believes my children to be perfect. With a family of seven, four daughters, Carrie, Rockie, Tammy, and Patty, and our son, there was the normal fighting and such. However, Carrie is different. She dotes on her little brother and even takes her younger sisters along with her to play. Carrie loves to play ball with her siblings and friends. They make quite the team. Carrie's church is also important to her. She loves the youth group. I remember how excited she was the night of the youth cantata. She had one of the leading roles, and had spent hours practicing to get it perfect. The cantata went great. The young peoples' dedication, hard work, and faith were evident.

Little did Carrie know how greatly this faith would be tested in the time to come. The faith of the rest of us, her family, would also be tested. As I looked around and thought about Carrie, I praised God and thanked Him for giving her to us for fifteen years. I found that with my own strength, I could not even walk in, but relying on God's grace I could walk in and also could praise Him right in the middle of a very grave situation. God's grace is truly sufficient.

CHAPTER 3
ONE DAY AT A TIME

"So don't be anxious about tomorrow. God will take care of your tomorrow, too. Live one day at a time" (Matthew 6:34; *Living Bible*).

At one o'clock that morning I was roused out of sleep by the telephone ringing. It was our pastor calling to tell me that the hospital wanted me to come back because Carrie had begun bleeding internally. He picked me up, and as we drove to the hospital the words of a song that talked about taking one day at a time, kept running through my mind. Upon arrival Charles told us that the doctor had said she couldn't make it through the night because she was bleeding faster than they could give her blood. However, by the time we arrived the bleeding had slowed and she was again holding her own. Since a recent case of the flu had caused her much stomach trouble, we thought that perhaps something related to it might have been causing the bleeding.

Much to the doctor's surprise, Carrie did live until morning; but now their backs were against the wall. Carrie was too weak for an operation to find the cause of the bleeding, yet if they didn't at least try to operate she would certainly bleed to death. Not seeing any other choice, they asked permission to operate. The doctors said they would rather go down trying than stand and watch her bleed to death. We agreed. Now, in an effort to prepare us for the worst by again assuring us that Carrie couldn't live through it, they took her into surgery. Our response to the doctor who took her was, "Do your best, but she is in God's hands."

Against all odds, Carrie lived through the surgery. I will never forget the stressful look on the surgeon's face as he came out from the operating room. He was completely worn out, yet also a little surprised. He told us that she had made it through the surgery and was stable. The doctor later commented to our pastor, "Your medicine is stronger than mine. I couldn't have pulled her through."

After the surgery Charles and I walked outside for some fresh air. It was then that I faced the whole future at once and fell apart. Most of Carrie's stomach had been removed, and yet the doctors could find nothing wrong except perfo-rations (holes in the stomach) caused by the stress of the coma. In other words, as far as they knew all of this was caused by the diabetes. I thought, *"She's still a diabetic. What next? How much more can she lose? Even if we get her home, maybe she'll be back in a month. Maybe next time it will be a lung or kidney or her sight."* I could just picture her dying one piece at a time. Yet in my spirit I felt sure she was going to live. My sister-in-law stated well how I felt when she said, "I don't believe you could kill the kid if you tried." It seemed as if God was protecting her supernaturally.

As I stood there believing Carrie would live but wonder-ing what the future would mean for her, I fell apart, again weeping uncontrollably. When I told a friend about this later, she commented, "God doesn't give grace for the whole future-only for today." Then I understood. That's what the Holy Spirit had been trying to teach me through the song about taking one day at a time. God knew I would foolish-ly face Carrie's entire future at once and fall apart, and He had tried to prepare me for it. I hadn't listened and fallen apart.

CHAPTER 4

NOT OUR DECISION

"And not only so, but we glory in tribulations also, knowing that tribulation worketh patience; And patience, experience; and experience, hope; And hope maketh not ashamed..." (Romans 5:3-5 KJV).

The day after the surgery Carrie remained stable, but as Charles talked to the surgeon he learned the total hopelessness of the case. Her body had quit producing protein and was very badly swollen. Now the surgeon made this statement, "We've kept her body alive with the use of machines, but she'll never come off the machines. She will never move again. Her mind is gone. There is no hope."

Again Charles and I walked outside the hospital. It was a beautiful spring day and somehow in the warmth of the sunshine the gloom seemed to lessen. As we sat down and began talking, we discovered that we both had been praying that this day would never happen-the day when we were told Carrie would never come off the machines. Although this thought probably hadn't crossed the doctor's mind, we thought he was saying, "It will come to a place where someone will have to decide whether to keep the machines on and keep her alive, perhaps for years in a coma, or shut the machines off and let her die."

During our discussion we agreed that God would not force us to make that decision. He loves us too much and He promised He would not give us over and above what we could handle, and that would be over and above. God holds the keys of life and death; not us or the doctors or any man, so we prayed and asked Him to make this decision, and we believed He would. God would take her or leave her, but the decision was His to make.

Together we found a great peace in knowing God was in charge; our hope was in Him. "And hope maketh not ashamed." It couldn't have been more than a minute after we finished praying that Charles' sister came out and eagerly stated, "She moved!" Knowing Carrie was in God's hands, we decided to go home, wash some clothes, get cleaned up and rest.

We had been home only about five minutes when the phone rang. It was Charles' sister calling from the hospital to let us know she was bleeding once again. As far as we were concerned, this was the end. If she continued bleeding there was nothing that could be done. On our way back to the hospital, I faced the fact that if Carrie lived it might be either in a brain dead state or with severe brain damage. I had previously faced the possibility of losing her, but the thought of brain damage just kept creeping into the back of my mind. I figured I would face that situation when the time came, if it did.

Now I seemed to hear God saying, "Face it. If it's brain damage or years in a coma, are you willing to accept it?" In the back of my mind was the thought that we might take Carrie home, perhaps with the mind of a two year old or less, to finish out her life in this way, or have to leave her somewhere to lie in a coma for years. I searched my heart on this. I counted the cost. Would I really be able to accept it, not only for Carrie, but the change it would bring into my family's life and mine?

Then I made my decision and in my heart I cried out, "Oh, yes, my God! If it be possible let this cup pass from me, but not my will but Thine be done. Yes Father, if you will be the most glorified through this by her having brain damage or lying for years in a coma, I will accept it. I want whatever will glorify you the most. My life and my family belong to you. Do as you will with them. But Lord, if this is what you need, you'll have to do it. I won't be able to, my family won't be able to, and if Carrie knows any of what's happening she won't either, but I know you will give me and my family the grace to handle this." I don't believe God is glorified because someone is ill, but I do believe He is glorified through the grace He gives us to handle the crisis situations that come into our lives.

I want to stop here to clarify several statements I make in this book. At times I say, "Heard God say, God seemed to be saying, or God said." I want to share with you that God has never talked audibly to me. However, when I am praying and fellowshipping with Him and studying His Word, He speaks in my mind through the Holy Spirit. "He will guide you into all truth" (John 16:13 KJV). He speaks through His Word, situations in my life (such as opened and closed doors), and just knowing in my heart that something is right. In the above instance it was simply a realization that I had faced every other way this illness might go, and in each case I was willing to accept God's will. Now He wanted me to face the possibility of having a brain damaged child. Would I be willing to trust God if Carrie lived in a brain damaged state for the rest of her life? Jesus put it this way, "My sheep hear my voice and I know them and they follow me" (John 10:27 KJV). God leads us in many different ways. However, we do have many definite promises in His Word that He will lead us if we look to Him.

When we arrived at the hospital, we learned the bleeding had slowed and Carrie was again holding her own. Our pastor arrived moments after we did and began praying for total healing. I really don't know how to explain what happened as he prayed, but I felt a real peace. We were back to praying for what God wanted. Charles and I had almost given up, but God wanted us to continue praying and trusting Him for healing. As the pastor prayed, I knew Carrie would be all right. Satan was to contest this many times in later days, but this was my first assurance of her complete healing.

CHAPTER 5

HAD I ONLY BEEN TOLD

"I will lift up mine eyes unto the hills. From whence cometh my help? My help cometh from the Lord, who made heaven and earth" (Psalms 121:1-2 KJV)

As I stood next to Carrie's bed looking at her, how thankful I was that she is a Christian. Carrie had received Christ during a youth rally in a week of revival meetings, but at that time she did not have enough courage to go forward in church for baptism. Shortly after this rally we discovered she was diabetic. Her Sunday school teacher sent her a card with this message written in, "God can help you more than anyone. Ask Him." I noticed Carrie read it and then laid it down sharply, as if angry. Although she accepted the disease very well, I had noticed she continually became upset if God was mentioned to her.

One day I asked her about this and she started crying and sobbed, "I don't want to talk about it." I continued to pray for her, and a few weeks later she went forward in church. She told me later that she had received Christ in the rally, but didn't have the courage to walk down the aisle in front of all those people. She confessed that, "The Lord kept working on me and I kept refusing to go. It finally came to the place where all I could hear was the verse, 'If you deny me before man, I will deny you before My Father in heaven.' I could hardly eat or sleep until I knew I had to go."

What a relief it was for Carrie when she finally was able to walk down the church aisle and to openly admit she had received Christ as her Savior. I quickly saw the evidence of her decision to follow Christ in her life. Carrie overcame much of her shyness and was becoming a leader. It was as if there wasn't anything that could keep her down. She was excited and enthusiastic about life. Being a very athletic person, Carrie had decided to become a gym teacher.

Now, if Carrie didn't pull through this illness, if she never spoke or walked again, I knew she would be in heaven and someday we would be joyously reunited. At this point I knew there was only one thing that was important. How many clothes she had, or what name brand they were, didn't seem important. Whether or not her clothes were hanging, which they probably weren't for she was a typical teen and they were probably scattered around the room, was not important. How nice her room looked wasn't important either, nor was how many friends she had or how well she had done in school. The only thing important now was whether or not Carrie was ready to meet God-and she did know Christ as her Savior and Lord.

As I stood there next to Carrie's bed, I couldn't help but wonder, *"How many children are not ready, how many are not saved?"* Thinking back to my own childhood, I know I would not have been ready to meet God even though I was raised in a Christian home; yet I can remember so desperately wanting to be a child of God.

The first time I remember seriously thinking about the Lord was when I was about five or six years old. That morning in Sunday school I heard the beautiful story of David and Goliath, and I was awed at the power and majesty of David's God. At the time, we attended a small town church where it was the custom to have a child who had memorized the Bible verse stand and recite it during the worship service. That morning I was the child chosen, and

I remember standing tall and proud and reciting, "I will lift up mine eyes unto the hills. From whence cometh my help? My help cometh from the Lord, who made heaven and earth" (Psalms 121:1-2 KJV).

When I sat down that morning, I listened carefully to the sermon and remember thinking, *"How great God must be! I wish He were my God. I wish I belonged to Him."* I believe with all my heart if someone had explained that God loves each of us, that He wants each one of us to belong to Him, and explained what I needed to do; I would have jumped at the chance. But apparently the message of salvation was not in the message that morning, or it was not given in a way I could understand. An invitation to receive Christ was never given in that church and I didn't know what to do about these feelings. I knew they would think I was much too young to receive Christ as my Savior, for I had seen them turn away older children than I. Knowing there wouldn't be any point in my asking about this, I just let it pass.

The next time I remember seriously thinking about God-looking back now I know I was under conviction-I was eleven years of age and still attended the church that taught you weren't held accountable for your sins until you turned twelve, so I thought, "I've got another year. I'll find out about this later, but not now." What a dangerous, dangerous attitude! The Bible tells us, "Now is the accepted time." I believe one of the saddest phrases spoken throughout all eternity by the lost will be, "I thought I had plenty of time!"

Two years passed before I remember thinking about God again. While I was attending a beautiful church camp located in the Rocky Mountains, I again started thinking about God. This camp had many activities for us campers; crafts, horseback riding, swimming, mountain hiking, and plenty of boys. I was having a wonderful time! One evening near the end of the week as we were sitting around the camp fire, I listened as several of the youth gave their testimonies. I could tell they had something I didn't and that old hunger to know God returned once again. I'm sorry to say this, but after thirteen years in church I still didn't know how to get God into my life. I'm not sure if the message of salvation wasn't taught in my church, or if there was such a lack of believing prayer for me that Satan was able to blind me from seeing it; whichever it was, at thirteen years of age, with a heart longing to know God, I still wasn't a Christian.

An invitation wasn't given that evening at the camp, and I didn't have the courage to stand up in front of all those kids and say, "Hey, tell me how I can get this." So I let it pass once again. I went to sleep that night thinking, *"I'm going to find out what this is all about in the morning. I don't care who I have to ask!"* The only explanation I can find for what happened next is found in Matthew 13:19 (NIV) which reads, "...when anyone hears the message about the Kingdom and does not understand it, the evil one comes and snatches away that which was sown in his heart. This is the seed sown along the path." I guess Satan snatched away the seeds, because the next morning I had forgotten all about my decision.

During the break that day, a friend and I went for a walk near the edge of camp. As we were walking we came upon a young counselor, probably high school or college age, and the subject of God came up. The young man made this statement, "You don't really believe in God, do you? I think He's a figment of someone's imagination. Weak people believe it because they need something to believe in. How do you know the Bible wasn't written a hundred or two years ago"?

After all those years in church but without any roots in Christ, I couldn't answer him. There's a famous evangelist who says, "If you ask someone to become a Christian, they'll always think of the worst Christian they know." That's just what I did. I thought of all those stories I had been taught about God's power and compared them with how powerless that "worst Christian" and some other professing Christians I knew seemed to be, and I thought, *"That would explain it. He's right. This is a bunch of junk they've been feeding me. There isn't any God."*

I went home from church camp that year an atheist; although I wouldn't have known what the word meant and would never have admitted it at the time. I soon found every excuse I could to skip church, including Sunday morning headaches.

I went to work soon after this-which involved working on Sunday-so I dropped out of church altogether. The only time I attended after that camp was on Sunday evening while dating Charles. He was one of those people who attended church Sunday evenings, and if I wanted to be with him, church was it. So, desiring to be with him and reasoning it couldn't hurt me, I went. But by now I was so sure that it was all a bunch of junk that I didn't even listen to the preacher. I looked around the building to check out what everyone else was wearing, who was with whom, watched the clock and thought, *"Isn't that preacher ever going to hush?"*

The only time I remember even feeling uncomfortable was during the invitation, not because I thought I might go forward, or even should, for I knew I wouldn't. I sat there and hoped no one else would, because as far as I was concerned if someone did they had made a public fool of themselves. What a shame after wanting God so badly as a child! It was years later, after marriage and four children, plus a lot of heartaches that I finally discovered the truth. It wasn't easy, and how I wish more of an effort had been made to win me to the Lord when I was a child and wanting to know Him so desperately. I wasted so many years seeking material possessions. Charles and I had a lot of things, but I was never satisfied. I was always seeking for something more without even realizing what it was.

Each of us has been created with emptiness in our hearts, a void which can only be filled with God. A person can never be truly happy until there is a personal relationship with God through receiving Christ, but I didn't know this. I kept thinking, *if we could just get this house finished! If we could just have this or that! If . . . if . . . if . . .* But as each of the "ifs" were filled, they brought only temporary joy.

One day I decided Charles was the cause of all my problems. Poor Charles! We always like to put the blame on others, don't we? I told him I wanted a divorce. He said, "No, that's not the answer." He explained that he had always wanted a little land in the country, and maybe if we could purchase some he would enjoy staying home more and we could work things out. Grabbing for straws, as it were, we listed our house in town for sale and bought a small farm.

This did help a little, but not much. I loved the country too, and this gave me a way to get out and walk or work off the tension, but the emptiness was still there. What was life all about? Surely this wasn't all there was to it. This had been our last hope.

We truly do take our feelings out on those around us, at least I did. The more miserable I became, the more I took it out on my children. My temper had always been a nasty one, and even though I tried to keep it under control, I found it beyond me. It's hard to be kind and cheerful when you're so miserable and unsettled yourself, and so I usually failed. One particularly bad day, after moving to the farm, I stopped and took a good hard look at my life, myself, my children, and my relationship with my husband. I didn't like what I saw. In fact, it made me sick to my stomach. This wasn't the kind of wife or mother I wanted to be. My children could do one of two things, they could become the kind of children who cower in the corner, afraid to move, or they could rebel, and they were doing some of both.

I soon found myself thinking that if my life ended, no matter what became of my children, they would be much better off. It couldn't be worse than this. So at the age of 28, with four children ten years old and under, I decided to end it all. I even planned the way. I was going to leave the children at my mother-in-law's and then proceed to drive off a high river bridge near our home. As I look back now, the fear that stopped me is almost ironic. I wasn't afraid of hell because I had convinced myself it didn't exist, and if it did I had decided that it couldn't be any worse than my life. Wow! I would have found out, wouldn't I? It scares me now to think of how close I came to finding out hell is real.

What stopped me from committing suicide that day was the fear that I might not be killed, but instead might end up as nothing more than what some people might refer to as a mummy-physically alive but mentally dead. I remember thinking what it would do to a family to have a member lying in a coma. I knew it would tear my family apart. I loved my family too much to take this chance, so I was stuck. I couldn't live and I couldn't die.

Then one night when Charles was gone-after I had gotten on to the kids and put them to bed early-I walked around the house and sat down on a pile of lumber and thought, If

I could just get this house finished, but I stopped myself cold and short, for I knew better than that. I just moved from a nice home and it hadn't made me happy.

Even though I had convinced myself God didn't exist, I must have known deep down that He did because as I sat down on that pile of lumber I cried out to Him, "Oh, my God! What is wrong with my life?"

One of the most wonderful things about God is that no matter how low you've sunk, He loves you so much that if you will take just one little step toward Him, He'll come all the rest of the way to you. I knew immediately what was wrong with my life. I had answered my own question. I had left God out.

Although to my knowledge I had not reviewed that verse I had recited in church as a child for twenty-two years, at this time it came back to me word perfect, "I will lift up mine eyes unto the hills. From whence cometh my help? My help cometh from the Lord." I knew that He was my answer. My help had to come from the Lord. I had to get back into church. I had to find out what this was all about; but Satan wasn't going to let it be easy. Back came the Sunday morning headaches and excuses-and by now I was good at making excuses for not attending church.

The Bible teaches there is a place we can go beyond where God will not strive with us any longer. In other words, He gives up on us; we've had our last chance. Even though I was only 28 years old, I believe I had almost reached that place. I didn't even know the Bible taught this, yet deep inside I began to realize if I didn't begin attending church and find out what God was all about, soon, I never would.

One Sunday morning I made up my mind. It was already too late to go to church that day, but I told my husband, "I don't know what you're going to do next Sunday, but I'm taking the girls and I'm going to church." When the following Sunday arrived, I did just that; but this time I went to his denomination and not the one I was raised in. A short time later the Lord began convicting me that the way I had been treating my children was not only a sin against them, it was a sin against God as well.

So many people feel they're going to make it to heaven by their own good works. I imagine if you walked down the streets of your city today and asked everyone you met if they were going to heaven, one of the most common answers you would hear would be, "Oh, I expect so. I'm about as good as the next guy." You know what is wrong with that kind of thinking, don't you? The Bible tells us the next guy is not good enough either. It tells us, ". . . there is none righteous, no not one" (Romans 3:10 KJV). Romans 3:23 reads (KJV), "For all have sinned and come short of the glory of God." That means you, it means me, and it means every one of us. The slightest lie separates us from the Holy God. Romans 6:23 (KJV) goes on to teach us the result of that sin: "For the wages of sin is death." I knew I was lost, without hope. But praise God that verse doesn't stop there. It goes on to say, "But the gift of God is eternal life through Jesus Christ our Lord."

I'm not going to say I fully understood that scripture at that point, because I don't believe I did. I simply had a picture of Jesus dying on the cross for me, and I now understood that it was going to take me turning from my way to His. One Sunday morning our Sunday school teacher quoted the verse, "Now is the day of salvation, now is the accepted time." I thought, "Yes, Now is the time. Yes, God." It wasn't a long fancy prayer; it was a simple commitment between me and Him. God knew what it meant and so did I. I had tried my way and it hadn't worked; now I was willing to go His. I can't describe the peace and joy that flooded my soul when I finally turned my life over to God. I realize when some people receive Christ they don't have a large emotional experience, but just a realization of having taken this step, and that's okay. We're all different. Perhaps it was because I had gone so far the other way that I did have this type of an emotional experience. I felt as if a thousand pounds had been lifted from my shoulders. I had been set free. I was right with God and I knew it.

I told Charles when I got home that day, "I don't know about you, but I'm going to heaven and I'd kind of like to see you there." It might sound as if a testimony would end there, but it doesn't. A new life had begun. My testimony had just begun.

CHAPTER 6

SONGS AT MIDNIGHT

"And at midnight Paul and Silas prayed, and sang praises unto God; and the prisoners heard them" (Acts 16:25 KJV).

Songs at midnight, are they really possible? I remember how God taught me all things are possible with Him. I was a brand new Christian and very excited about it. I wanted to find out all I could about God. I had just found out He was very real. The day I received Christ, I picked up my Bible and started reading. To my disappointment, I found I didn't understand what it meant; so turning to God I said, "I didn't understand that, but you wrote it; you know what it means. Please help me understand it. Teach it to me."

As I continued to study and pray, God began to teach me the great truths of His Word. I had passed from death to life, all because of what Jesus had done for me. He was willing to hang on the cross to take the punishment for my sins. Because He shed His blood, I could be forgiven-and anyone else who would believe in Him. Then He was buried, but death had no hold over Him. He has risen! He is alive! I had invited Him into my heart and He is living in me. My heart sang with joy for all of my sins were forgiven.

As the weeks passed and I continued to study God's Word and pray, something began to bother me. What about the people around me, the ones who didn't know Jesus? They were lost and on their way to an eternal hell. Perhaps some of them wanted to know God, even as I had as a small child, and no one was telling them how to find Him. Many times I wept and prayed, "Please God, let me tell them. Let me keep them from making the same mistake I almost made. I'll go anywhere. I'll do anything. Here am I, send me."

I had found Christ, been baptized, and was now a member of a great church. One day the phone rang. It was the Sunday School Superintendent of this church. "I'm going to call on you for the closing prayer at the end of opening exercise this morning," he said.

"Who me? Pray in public! You must be kidding," I responded.

"No," he replied. "I'm going to call on you."

"I won't pray," I protested.

"If I called on you, you'd have to," he added.

"Oh, no I wouldn't," I insisted. "I could always get up and walk out."

Needless to say he didn't call on me, but the Lord really went to work. I could almost hear Him saying, "Oh, sure, you would go anywhere. You would do anything. Well, all except say one little prayer in public."

The Bible teaches very clearly that God will not give us the big tasks until we have proven faithful in the small. So I had to back up, confess that one as sin, and ask for another chance.

A few days later the superintendent's wife called. Praise the Lord for persistent people. They pushed me until I became frustrated. As I look back now I wonder if they hadn't have pushed, would I have gone? Praise the Lord they were persistent. His wife called and said, "I want you to give the devotion in our Circle."

After what had happened with her husband, I couldn't

say no. "Okay," I responded. Then I hung up the phone and almost died. "Lord, I can't do that. You know I can't do that. Sure they can, they've been Christians for years. I'm new at this. This isn't fair." Somehow though, even as I complained, I knew I had to do it. So finally, beaten and without an argument left, I sat down and picked up my Bible.

Lo and behold, the first words I read were, "I can do all things through Christ who strengtheneth me" (Philippians 4:13 KJV). God then took me through a set of verses He would use on me many times in the upcoming years. He moved me on to Galatians 2:20 (KJV), ". . . and yet not I, but Christ liveth in me." Then He continued with, "If God be for us who can be against us?" (Romans 8:31 KJV) and "With men this is impossible but with God all things are possible" (Matthew 19:26 KJV). Finally, God took me back to Moses at the burning bush. You know he sounded just like you and me today. "But Lord, I can't do that." Yet God commanded him, "Now go; I will help you speak and will teach you what to say (Exodus 4:12 NIV)"

From there He took me to Joshua. Can you imagine how Joshua felt as he looked at those huge walls of Jericho? He couldn't do anything about them, and he knew it because it was humanly impossible. But the Bible tells us he lifted up his eyes and prayed (Joshua 5:13). So I lifted up my eyes and prayed, "All right, Lord. I can do it. But you will have to do it through me, just as You did for Joshua and Moses."

I'll never forget the day I gave that devotion. There were all of five ladies present, but I was so scared I was shaking like a leaf. I had what I thought was a good devotion-at least the Lord had used it on me. I had it all written down and just more or less read it. One time during the entire presentation I mustered up enough courage to look up, and when I did I saw tears streaming down the faces of those dear saints. To this day I don't know whether they were crying because my devotion was that good or because they were praying so hard that God would just get me through it. He did, and I went home praising God that I had been counted worthy to suffer for Him.

He has since taught me that I truly can do all things through Christ. He never lets me down. I can do anything He asks. At the time of that first devotion I would never have dreamed I would one day be writing a book from a hospital room to shout this to the world.

It was not until several weeks later that I found the courage to pray in public. Several churches were meeting together for a special *World Day of Prayer* program, and I had agreed to read a part, but refused to close with prayer. However, when the day came and I finished my reading, I realized if I was going to follow Christ all the way, it was going to take obedience. I must be willing to do anything He asked. I knew He wanted me to close with prayer and refusing to do so would be disobeying Him, so I finished with, "Please close your eyes for prayer." It was short and probably very poorly worded, but it came from my heart in obedience, and I'm sure He blessed it.

The superintendent's wife told me later that she had been praying very hard for God to give me the desire and courage to close with prayer, and He had. I've heard being a Christian compared to an exciting mountain climbing adventure-an adventure that leads you to a glorious experience at the top. During the climb the view is breathtaking, and even though at times it gets rough, if you allow God to be your guide, it won't matter which path He takes you down, you will desire to join Paul and Silas singing praises to Him at midnight.

CHAPTER 7

FEED MY LAMBS

"Even so it is not the will of your Father, who is in heaven, that one of these little ones should perish" (Matthew 18:14; KJV).

Almost immediately after I became a Christian and began asking God to let me tell others about Him, I saw an article in the newspaper. It read, "Child Evangelism Teacher Training Class." The article went on to explain that the purpose of the class was to train teachers for Good News Clubs. I had never heard of Child Evangelism Fellowship or Good News Club, but I knew the lady who had put the article in the paper. She was one of my girls' Sunday school teachers and the class was to be in her home. I felt if there ever was a Spirit-filled person, she was it. Also, I knew what "child" and "evangelism" meant, and it sounded like a good idea.

So mostly on my faith in my friend, I called and asked her what a Good News Club was. Her answer was quite surprising. She said, "I don't know. Come and we'll find out together." She explained that she had worked in Junior Church in Kansas City with some individuals who were involved in Good News Clubs, and she felt led by the Lord to find out more about them. I told her I'd be there.

Again the devil didn't like it. The morning of the training I had everything from sick children to car trouble, so I simply prayed, "Well, Lord, I guess if you want me there you can work it out." He did, and I made it. By the time I left that training class I knew it was not only right, but this was where the Lord wanted me to work.

I'd like to share an experience from that class with you. How many of you teach? Now, how many of you think you know which of your students are listening? I saw the man who taught that class a couple years later and he confessed how he and his wife had talked about me on their way home. They were quite surprised I had taken the test and then continued on to teach the clubs. He said I had such a blank look on my face that they thought they had lost me. Yet far from not listening, the Lord was working so deeply in my heart that I didn't have anything to add. It is better not to give up on a person because you don't know their heart.

In case you're not familiar with Good News Clubs, they are interdenominational Bible clubs held wherever there is an open door-usually in homes. Their purpose is to reach the unreached child with the gospel and to make every effort to lead them to Christ, and to work for Christian growth in the saved child. After a child is reached for Christ, the teacher then makes every effort possible to get that child into a Bible believing church. These clubs meet at a time that is convenient for both the teacher and the hostess, and at a time when the children can come. Generally this is right after school, although sometimes it is on Saturdays or at night.

Many children are reached for Christ through Good News Clubs who would not be reached otherwise, mostly because there isn't any effort on the parents' part to make sure they hear the message of salvation. These clubs elim-inate the parents' excuses for not attending church, and they even give them an extra hour after school one day a week. The child whose parents would not make the effort to get them ready for church on Sunday-even if you offered to pick them up-will usually come with a friend to Good News Club where they hear about Jesus.

My friend and I took the training and began a club in our town, but something happened on one specific day that caused me to really become a Good News Club teacher. An eight year old little girl, who had never been to church in her life, started coming to club. At first she didn't even know who Jesus was, she had not heard about Him. She continued coming for several weeks. This day I was giving the Bible lesson. It was one of those days, not when you feel like you've lost the children's attention, but rather, that you never had it to begin with. Yet this little girl was different. She didn't take her eyes off me through the entire lesson and it was obvious that she was very much under conviction. When I gave the invitation that day, she raised her hand. The other teacher counseled with her and she prayed to receive Christ. Before she left she came up to me and said, "Mrs. Daffern, I knew I had sinned. I asked Jesus to forgive me and come into my heart." Then with tears streaming down her face and the biggest grin I think I've ever seen she added, "And I love Him so!"

If I live to be a hundred and see many people find Christ, the testimony of that little girl will be one of the greatest. That was the day I knew Good News Clubs really worked.

Yet the story doesn't end there. Before we moved away from Cherryvale, I was also blessed to see her make a public profession of faith in Christ at church and receive baptism. Soon after her public profession and baptism, her older sister also accepted Christ . . . followed by her mother. The last Sunday we attended that specific church, her father was with them. "A little child shall lead them."

CHAPTER 8

THE FIRE

"And He took a child, and sat him in the mist of them; and when He had taken him in His arms..." (Mark 9:36 KJV).

Some wonder if the conversion of so young a child is really genuine. Here's how the Lord convinced me. First read all of Matthew 18. Now note especially verse two, "And Jesus called a little child unto him and set him in the midst of them." Did you notice Jesus said a little child? How large of a child would you pick up and set in the midst of a group? Also, in Mark 9:36 we're told Jesus held this child in his arms. How many of you would hold a child of twelve in your arms? You wouldn't have mine, they were as big as I was by the age of twelve.

Now look at the sixth verse. "But whosoever shall offend one of these little ones who believe in me, it were better for him that a millstone be hanged about his neck and that he were drowned in the depth of the sea." This shows the seriousness of offending one of these little ones who believe.

I'd like to explain a little about these verses. The word used for "little ones" in Matthew 18:6 is the word "micros." It is the Greek word from which we get the English word "micro" which means exceedingly small or microscopic. Jesus was talking about a very small child here. Jesus settled forever the question of whether a little child can believe and be saved when He said, "little ones which believe in

Me." The words for "believe in me" are the same as used in John 3:16. Very certainly Jesus was talking about this little "micros" child as having a saving faith.

Isn't this the condition we must all reach to be saved; to believe in Jesus with a saving faith? I can't think of a greater way to offend a child who believes in Jesus than to tell them they're too young to come to Christ. God forgive us for the children who could have been reached, but weren't because we thought they were too young.

See also Mark 10:14, "But when Jesus saw it He was much displeased, and said unto them, permit the little children to come unto Me, and forbid them not; for of such is the kingdom of God." If Jesus said let them come to Him, do we dare refuse? Yes, I believe a child's decision is as genuine and lasting as an adult's. How can we dispute Jesus' word? If He said a little child can believe in Him, who are we to say they can't?

As for personal experience, I must admit that even after the training class I had some doubts about children as young as five, but the Lord used my own child to prove his truth to me. My youngest daughter, Patty, who was five at this time, came in one day and asked me about heaven and hell. She had spent the night with a friend and they had talked about them. After their discussion she was full of questions. I used all the knowledge I had just gained in the teacher training class to explain the way of salvation to her, but I still had doubts about her being old enough. Finally, I commented, "That's all I know to tell you." Apparently that was enough because a few minutes later she came bounding into the kitchen, smiling from ear to ear and saying, "Mamma, I did it! I did it!"

"Did what?" I questioned.

"I asked Jesus in."

Since then she has shown a great amount of Christian growth and even led several of her friends to the Lord. She doesn't have any doubts about her salvation. Jesus is very real to her.

Not long after Patty received Christ, she was standing near a big container where some trash was burning in our back yard. Somehow a spark blew out of the container and landed on her dress and it caught on fire. She was quite a distance from the house, and even if I had heard her scream, I couldn't have made it to her before she was severely burned. In her words, this is what happened: "I was scared! I didn't know what to do so I said, 'Jesus Help!' Then I knew to lie down and roll over." She came into the house with one badly ruined dress, but not a burn on her body.

One of the things God has most vividly impressed on me through this illness of Carrie's is that we must reach our children as children. Some of them may not have time to grow up.

CHAPTER 9

CRYING CHILDREN

"It is God himself, in His mercy, who has given us this wonderful work (of telling his Good News to others) and so we never give up" (2 Corinthians 4:1; TLB).

There is one miracle in my life that, because of the effect it might have on another, must remain a silent miracle. It is the way God taught me He is a God of miracles. He is over all government agencies and will answer the believing prayers of his children. Through this miracle, my faith in his absolute ability to do anything was established. Out of necessity, I will leave that miracle silent and go on with another experience.

I had been working in the Good News Club some time when God gave us a baby boy. Along with him, however, came another complication-that of taking a baby out with each trip to town. With the farm already taking its toll on us, financially and physically, and Charles working out of town most of the winter, I was left caring for the livestock. This caused a physical condition of mine to be greatly aggravated, and one problem was stacking up on top of another. Of course, God is able to work out our problems, but because they kept piling up and there didn't seem to be a way out, we began to wonder if He was trying to tell us something. Maybe God had plans for us other than this farm.

We began seeking God's will on this, praying and study-ing His word. One day as I was especially concerned about this situation, I came across a verse that really spoke to me. It said, "You've studied long enough; now go out and teach." "But Lord," I protested, "I'm teaching in two Good News Clubs, superintendent of the Beginner Department in Sunday school, and hold an office in both a circle and Women's Missionary Union. What more can I do?"

A few days later, while still wondering about this, another verse spoke to me, "And other sheep I have, that are not of this fold; them also I must bring . . ." (John 10:16 KJV). I realize this is talking about Jews and Gentiles, but as I read that passage that day it made me stop and think about the fact that God has a special place for us. I just didn't feel we were supposed to stay where we were. Because of this, plus several other incidents-and some plain common sense-Charles and I began to realize the farm was not God's plan for us anymore. With a prayer of, "Lord, if you want us to move, you'll have to sell this farm," we put it up for sale. It sold in less than two months, so now we had to find a place to move.

There were at least three possibilities. One was Cherryvale, which seemed the best place for the kids because they were already attending the school there, we loved the church, and the Good News Clubs were already established. This would have been our choice. The second town was Parsons, for Charles worked out of Parsons. The third choice was back to Independence. With three very reasonable options, we weren't sure where to move. All we knew was that we wanted to move to wherever the Lord wanted us.

As I looked back over the previous months, I was reminded of several things that had happened, all pointing to the fact that the Lord was finished with us in Cherryvale. First, I felt less of a need for my work in Cherryvale. My children had shared an epidemic of mumps and I had missed club for about six weeks. It had continued just fine without me. Next, at this same time I had become more and more burdened for the children in the nearby town of Independence, which was where we lived just prior to my becoming a Christian. As I mentioned before, at that point in my life I didn't even believe there was a God.

When we moved from Independence, several years earlier, we had left a circle of friends that I considered "quite uptown." We had gone many places together: coffees, parties, shopping, camping, etc. On Friday evening the men would gather together to play poker and the women and I would hire a baby-sitter and go out to eat. Then we returned to one of the homes where we would play games, fix hair, talk, or do whatever.

One Friday when we were playing *Double Jeopardy*, I picked the category of "The Bible" and shot through all five questions without hesitation, thereby proving a good knowledge of the Scriptures. Remember, I had been raised in church and had good head knowledge of the Scriptures.

After discovering my Bible knowledge, one of my friends asked what I thought about God. I knew she had recently started attending church, and guess what I did? I laughed and said, "You don't really believe in God do you? I think He's a figment of someone's imagination. Weak people believe it because they need something to believe in. How do you know the Bible wasn't written a hundred or two years ago?" Wow! The exact same words the counselor used on me. Needless to say, she stopped attending church.

After becoming a Christian and finding out how real God is, I remembered the comment that I had made to this friend. I knew how Simon Peter felt when he denied Jesus. And like him, I wept and asked God to please let me change my

45

testimony. Now I found myself really praying for her and her children, wondering if they could be reached for God through a Good News Club. More and more it seemed the Lord was leading us to Independence. Finally, it came to the point where we had to make up our mind. We had ruled out Parsons, so we called a real estate agent we knew would look in either Independence or Cherryvale and made an appointment.

The night before the appointment we still weren't sure, but felt it was Independence. I would be moving for the purpose of starting Good News Clubs in Independence. After all the Lord had taught me, you may be surprised to know what I said. "But Lord, I can't do that. Sure my friend could, but she's friendly and outgoing. I've always found it hard to talk to people." So God took me back through all those verses He had already taught me, until I finally admitted, "All right, Lord, I can."

God then reminded me of the verse that reads, "How can he go unless he is sent?" At that point I took that to mean I couldn't go unless God sent me. "All right," I agreed, "I'll go; but Father, I must know for sure this is your plan. If it's mine, if for any reason I just want to do it, you and I both know it will fall flat on its face; but if it's yours, there won't be any holding it back. If this is your idea, God, please give me a call to Independence."

Leaving it in God's hands, I went to bed. That night while Charles was still in the other room, I had a very strange experience. I wasn't anywhere near asleep. I was just lying there thinking this through, when suddenly it seemed as if I were in a place waiting for someone to receive instructions as to what to do with me. I couldn't see anything, I just remember waiting. Then I was being transported somewhere. I still couldn't see a thing, but I was aware of the presence of two beings-as I look back I suppose they were angels. They sat me down on a platform which was similar to a stage. I felt as the prophet when he said, "There remained no strength in me." I wanted to run, but couldn't. As I looked up, I witnessed a vast number of children surrounding me. With one voice they chorused, "We're lost! We're lost! We're lost! Independence! Independence! Independence!" Then just as fast as it all happened, it was over.

I remembered the verse, "take off your shoes, for the ground on which you stand is Holy ground." If I had been wearing shoes I would have taken them off. The presence of God filled that room in a way I had never experienced before or since. Then He touched me and I felt all my weakness drain out and his strength replace it. There was no doubt. We were going to Independence; not on our own strength, but on His. Then in my mind I heard the words, "Go in peace my child."

"Okay, Lord," I whispered. "And I'm going to expect miracles over and above what I can ever hope or think." Independence, here we come!

CHAPTER 10

WALK BY FAITH

"For we walk by faith, not by sight" (2 Corinthians 5:7 KJV).

One of the first things God taught me in Independence was the importance of one child. He says, "It is not my will that even one of these little ones perish." Too many times we get hung up on numbers. Yes, numbers are important, but I believe one of the worst mistakes we can make as Christians is to look up to the one with large numbers and down on the one with few. Remember, God called Philip away from a huge revival to reach one soul. Many times we're tempted to feel if our work isn't "big" then it isn't accomplishing what it should.

I almost fell into that trap when I started a Good News Club in my home in Independence. I struggled to motivate children to come. Then through a phone call one day, I was offered another home in which to begin a club. Filled with joy and excitement, I started my second club, only to find the same struggle. Although we were accomplishing much and decisions to receive Christ were being made, I didn't think the clubs were as large as they should be.

The next winter I had an opportunity to start a third club. I stalled for a while thinking, *"Why bother? The ones we have aren't doing what they should."* One day a Christian friend made a statement that was to change my mind. She was not talking about Good News Club but about her own work when she said, "As Christians we do not walk by sight but by faith."

I knew she was right, so I called the one who had offered to be a hostess and said, "Let's get started." I was claiming Isaiah 55:11 (KJV), ". . .so shall my word be that goeth forth out of my mouth; it shall not return unto me void, but it shall accomplish that which I please, and it shall prosper in the thing whereto I sent it." I still didn't know if we would have large numbers, but I felt if one child found Christ through her club, it would be worth it.

It was no more than a couple of weeks later when the Lord made me another fabulous promise. While reading my Bible one day a verse became more of a personal promise to me than any other Scripture ever had. It seemed as if it were a direct promise from God, as if it were written for me alone. It was Revelation 3:8 (KJV), "I know thy works; behold I have set before thee an open door, and no man can shut it; for thou hast a little strength and hast kept my word, and hast not denied my name."

Does God keep his promises? I believe He does. Yet it looked like my troubles had just begun. Not only did we continually seem to have this fight with numbers-we would build up, drop down, build up, drop down, anywhere from 48 to 2-I also had a hard time finding help. I was teaching three Good News Clubs, the lesson in Jr. Church, I held an office in a Circle or Women's Missionary Group or both, and had a family of seven. I found myself with not nearly enough time and energy.

Try as I would, it seemed a never-ending battle to secure helpers who were dedicated and willing to invest their time and hearts into the clubs. I believe God usually directs a person who is going to teach his Word to take the time necessary to prepare in study and prayer. If someone is not willing to take time to adequately prepare (when they know ahead of time they are going to teach), then they need to forget it.

It was extremely difficult to find a helper willing to spend the time and effort required, and to continue the work and believe when the going got rough. I'll never forget arriving at club one day only to have no one show up- teacher or pupil. I loaded everything back into the car and started to leave. As I prepared to leave, two children arrived. They were children of members of our church. I knew they lived in the country and the mother would have to stay in town and wait for them with a younger child, so I canceled club that day.

On the way home, I faced the fact that there might not be anyone willing to go with me on this, but I made a commitment to God. "Heavenly Father," I prayed. "Though none go with me, still I will follow." You send me one child to teach and I'll teach, but it's hard going alone."

He wrapped his arms around me and I heard him say, "I know, child."

Then I added, "But not as hard as it was for Jesus to hang on the cross for me."

The next week we had 17 children in that club.

CHAPTER 11

A CAT

"Submit yourselves, therefore, to God. Resist the devil, and he will flee from you" (James 4:7 KJV).

One day we had an exceptionally large group of children for the Good News Club at my home. They were also a particularly restless group, and I was having trouble maintaining order and keeping their attention. As we began the Bible lesson, they seemed to settle down fairly well.

Then the interruptions began! First the phone rang. After this situation was handled, it took a while to settle the children back down. Almost as soon as they were calmed, there was a knock on the door. It was a lady with the new phone books. After another settling down period and they were once again listening, our parakeet escaped from his cage. He loved attention, and when he discovered the children would squeal if he flew over their heads just missing them, his reign of terror began-totally disrupting the club. We eventually caught him and put him back in his cage.

Once more when the children were finally quieted and listening, I heard a scratching noise, looked up, and there was a cat climbing the screen of the living room window. The Bible gives many descriptions of the devil, but as far as I was concerned at that moment there was only one-he looked like a cat.

My first thought was that I might as well quit, but as the Lord checked me I thought, *Now wait a minute. That's what Satan wants!* I have found many times that when Satan works the hardest against you, that's when you have the most results. So I commanded, "Satan! Oh, no you don't. I know you're powerful, but 'greater is He that is in me than He that is in the world.' The Lord is far more powerful than you and you are a defeated foe." I continued, "God, I draw nigh to you. Satan, I resist you in the name of Jesus. You will no longer be able to harass this club. Lord, I am asking for and counting on your divine protection for the rest of this club. Kids, let's go on with the lesson."

When I gave the invitation that day, a little girl raised her hand indicating she wanted to receive Christ. As I counseled with her she said, "I have been in Sunday school all my life and heard about Jesus, but I never realized until today that I have never made a decision to receive Him myself. I want to do that today."

Wow! That's what Good News Club is all about. Praise the Lord; He kept me going even when it got rough. Our pastor has a favorite saying, "If you haven't met the devil today, maybe it's because you're running with him." Another way I've heard it said is, "If Satan isn't contesting what you're doing, maybe you better quit and do something worthwhile."

Yes, he does give you a rough time if you are a threat to him. It is a bad mistake for a Christian to under- estimate the power Satan can usurp. Never forget though, God is greater. If you are in Christ, as far as you are concerned, Satan is a defeated foe. You already have the victory. All you need to do is claim it and then walk in it.

CHAPTER 12

GOD-GIVEN APPOINTMENTS

'Let us therefore, come boldly unto the throne of grace that we may obtain mercy, and find grace to help in time of need" (Hebrews 4:16 KJV).

Soon after the time when no one came to Good News Club, the hostess and I became very burdened to begin a prayer band. I had tried to begin one earlier, but had not been able to interest anyone in coming. Now there were three of us desiring to pray for the clubs. The Bible says two or more, so we set a day to meet and begin praying.

The morning we were to initiate the prayer band it seemed as if everything went wrong. Just as I began to get David and myself ready to go, the phone rang. This, of course, caused me to be running late. As soon as I hung up, I excitedly stated, "David, come on. Let's hurry." David was two years old.

We went rushing up the stairs and he fell. His nose was crooked and began bleeding profusely. I picked him up and tried to stop the bleeding, but it was useless. When I reached my bedroom, I sat down on the bed with him in my arms and prayed, "Father, I believe this is Satan's work. He doesn't want us to begin this prayer band. If the key person (this is my official title) doesn't show up, it isn't going to happen." As I touched his nose I said, "I'm going to ask you to touch David and stop the bleeding and fix his nose. I ask this in Jesus' name. Amen." Immediately the bleeding stopped. A strange look came upon his face and he instantly stopped crying. When I examined his nose closer, it was completely straight. The prayer band was started that day. Many times there were only two or three people there, but that's okay. It fulfilled the condition made in the Bible.

This isn't the only experience I've had with God meeting needs in the form of healing. Many times He has taken care of physical problems for me as well as others for whom I have prayed. Once before, when Carrie was in the hospital, I had quite an experience along this line. I figured since God had put me in that hospital room, He must have something for me to do. I began praying that He would show me what it was, and it wasn't long before I knew.

There was an elderly lady staying in the room with Carrie. She was suffering with pneumonia, seemed to be in a lot of pain and was very discouraged. I knew she was one of the reasons I was there when she told her granddaughter she didn't care if she lived or died. With that kind of attitude, and a severe case of pneumonia, her prognosis didn't look good. She had been there quite awhile without any improvement. I started praying, "All right, Lord. Show me how I can help her."

My first thought was to tell her about Jesus. "But Lord, I can't do that," I thought, "I don't even know her."

Surprisingly, it seemed as if God was saying, "I don't want you to." I thought, "Now wait a minute, Lord. Let's be sure we understand each other. Here's a lady, very possibly dying, and I don't know if she's ready or not to meet you and you don't want me to tell her how to receive Christ as her Savior."

"That's what I said," He answered as He worked through my thoughts and his word. A period of silence followed. Then He seemed to say, "All I want you to do is to be willing to let me do what I want through you."

How foolish I was. Jumping right into thinking I had to do it. I wondered at God's patience. How many times He had taught me I couldn't do anything. My righteousness is as filthy rages. Have you ever considered that verse? It doesn't say our sins are as filthy rags, it says our very best, our righteousness is as filthy rags. I said, *"Okay, Lord. I'm willing. "*

As soon as I prayed that prayer I began approaching the problem from a different angle. The Lord knew what needed to be done, and I found myself thinking, *"What would Jesus do? Of course! He would approach her with love. But how Lord? How can I show her love? "*

I thought of all the people who had been in to pray for Carrie. No one seemed to care that much for this lady, but Jesus did. I knew He wanted to pray for her through me.

Being a firm believer in the use of the Scripture, I stopped and asked God what scripture He wanted me to use. He reminded me of Hebrews 4:16. By this time she had turned her back toward me. I couldn't tell if she was asleep, and didn't want to wake her if she was finally resting, so I simply prayed, *"Lord, show me when. "* Just then she turned around and looked at me. After sharing the scripture with her, I asked, "Would it be all right if I prayed for you?"

"I guess it would be okay," she murmured.

I left soon after praying for her, for I had walked and it was getting dark outside. The next day when I went in to see Carrie, her roommate was sitting on the edge of the bed with a big smile on her face. "How do you feel?" I asked.

"I feel fine," she replied. "I haven't coughed all night. What church do you attend?"

We talked quite a while and I discovered she was a Christian but had not been in church for many years and needed encouragement. She had been having many difficulties with her family, so I shared some scriptures which related to family with her. The next morning the doctor told her she could go home in a few days-and I wouldn't be at all surprised if she went to church as soon as possible.

CHAPTER 13

TROUBLED WATERS

"But a child left to himself brings his mother to shame" (Proverbs 29:15 KJV).

Because I needed help so badly in the Good News Clubs, I finally decided to step out in faith and set up a teacher training class. I believe God meets our needs, and I considered this a need, so I was sure He would meet it. When the day of the class came, the attendance was fair. However, when it was over, only one person said she would finish the year with the club in her home. Since I had just lost one teacher, that still left me with three clubs to teach. I was terribly upset. I felt as though I was not spending enough time with my family, and yet I didn't want to drop a Good News Club.

How do you go to a group of children-some of them new Christians from non-Christian homes who have come to learn God's Word-and say, "Don't come next week? There won't be anyone here to teach you?" I didn't know what to do. I was torn between family and clubs, feeling one was my responsibility and one God's calling. I felt God had let me down. I'd given all I had to Him and to these clubs, and now it seemed they were finished.

While washing dishes one afternoon, I was talking to God about this. "Heavenly Father," I prayed. "I know this is a wrong attitude, but I can't seem to help it. I know you know about it anyway, so we might as well work it out. I feel you've let me down. You've promised to meet my needs, and I needed a teacher. What happened? I know you love me. Please help me with this attitude. I can't face doing those clubs next week. I am too tired. I just can't do it, and with this attitude I won't help them or me. Please help me. I ask this is Jesus' name. Amen."

Would you believe it started snowing? It continued snowing until finally the radio announced that the buses would not run the next day. My Monday hostess called to find out what we were going to do about club. Most of the children attending the club in her home lived in the country and rode the bus. Since Carrie was sick and I didn't feel I should leave her, I said, "I guess we'll have to cancel club." She agreed to call the children and let them know of our decision.

I had just hung up the phone when the Tuesday's hostess called. She reported that three members of her family had bad cases of the flu and were running high fevers, and therefore we would have to cancel club. She graciously agreed to call the children also.

This left only the one at my house on Thursday. I figured I could handle one club and was very relieved, although it later was canceled due to Carries' illness. Again, I could almost hear God say, "Do you see how much I love you? I would cause a snowstorm for you."

That settled it for that week, but the struggle for a permanent solution went on. One day while doing dishes-seems I'm always doing dishes-and thinking about what scripture to have in our prayer meeting that afternoon, it hit me, "There is always an answer." All you have to do is ask God, believe He'll answer, and look for it. "If you want to know what God wants you to do, ask Him, and He will gladly tell you, for He is always ready to give a bountiful supply of wisdom to all who ask Him; He will not resent it"

(James 1:5: TLB). Sharing this scripture as well as others on the subject with Pat, one of my prayer partners, I told her all we need to do is believe and obey. "I'm going to do it today," I announced.

Before we even began to pray the answer came. I answered my own question when I made this statement, "If my own family is not honoring to God, what I say in these clubs means nothing. Then I remembered, "A child left to himself brings his mother to shame" (Proverbs 29:15). I realized this verse is talking about discipline, but you can't discipline a child if they're home alone much of the time and you haven't any idea what they're doing. This is the same as leaving them to themselves.

I knew this was my answer. I was to give up all the clubs except the one in my own home. This one club would not mean leaving my own children alone, yet would also give them extra spiritual instruction. I was sure the Lord would allow it. I didn't understand these instructions, but I believe as in the case of Saul (1 Samuel 13:13), whether we understand a situation or agree with it, once we know God's instructions we had better obey.

I told Pat, "I'm going to close out the clubs as soon as possible this year, and then next fall I will have only the one in my own home." I felt bad about it in a way, like God had taken my ministry away; but I did it anyway. As soon as this decision was made public, I realized God had not taken my ministry away, but had only perfected it.

I know many young mothers have received the same message I have on my family. If America is to be straightened out, we mothers-whenever possible-must return to our own homes and start raising our children instead of just letting them grow up on their own. I believe if you will ask God about this yourself and do as He leads, if He leads you to stay home with your children He will make your husband able to financially support your family. Perhaps He will enable you to help in a way that will allow you not to leave your children. If you have to work outside of the home, make sure to spend the time you have off work with your children. Spend time with your family. Take them to church. Pray with them. Teach them the scriptures.

When your family is the way God wants them to be, it becomes his responsibility to make sure your needs are met. Some would say, "But He didn't meet your needs for a teacher." But, there's more to this story.

As I thought about this, I realized how perfect it was. All these mothers willing to obey God and finding themselves with extra time at home-what a setup! If even a few of them answered God's call on Good News Club and began reaching the children, think how much more they could do than I alone, and I wouldn't be neglecting my own family.

CHAPTER 14

ONLY RESPONSIBLE FOR SELF

"For the battle is not yours but God's" (2 Chronicles 20:15 KJV).

A nother important lesson I learned at this same time is that each of us is only responsible for doing what God wants us to do. One Sunday in Jr. Church, I gave the story of Jehoshaphat (2 Chronicles 20) and ended the lesson with this statement, "How many of you griped and complained last week? That was sin. God gave us a definite way to work out problems and it wasn't through griping and complaining."

Later that day a problem came my way. Guess what I did? You're right! I griped and complained. We had a family problem and being very unhappy about it, I stormed upstairs. Once upstairs, the Holy Spirit began to convict me and I remembered the statement I had made in Jr. Church. I told God, *"But Lord, this is different."*

"Is it?" He questioned. Well, of course, I had to admit it wasn't and confess it as sin. Then He reminded me of the pattern for problems in the lesson. King Jehoshaphat was frightened when he discovered that a mighty army was coming against Judah. The Bible reads, "He feared." However, being a man of God, he knew what to do about it. He set himself to seek the Lord. He proclaimed a fast and called the people together and began praising the Lord. They remembered God's greatness and how He had helped them in the past.

Now, I certainly didn't feel much like praising the Lord at that point. However, He said in his Word that this was the first step in solving a problem, so I was determined to obey whether my feelings agreed or not. So I began praising the Lord.

Then God took me on to the next step. Jehoshaphat told God the problem and then asked for help. I really appreciated this. So many times we're told to just praise the Lord, and of course this is right, but God went on to reveal that He wants us to tell Him our troubles and ask for His help. This is what I did. I poured out my heart to Him. I had good reason to be concerned over this matter. It wasn't a solution selfishly desired, but rather a matter which would glorify Him and bring people to Him.

At that point, I knew more than ever before what God wanted for my family. *"All right, Lord," I prayed. "You do whatever you need to do. Use any or all members of this family, and put us where you want us."* Don't pray this unless you mean it!

The next step in the story of Jehoshaphat was God's answer, and I knew it was mine also. "Be not afraid or dismayed by reason of this great multitude, for the battle is not yours but God's." Now praise for the Lord poured forth from my heart. This wasn't my battle, it was God's. My part was simply obeying Him myself.

CHAPTER 15

RIGHT WITH GOD

"He who conceals his sins does not prosper" (Proverbs 28:13; NIV).

Along with the struggle in attendance and helpers in Good News Club, I faced several other trials in my life. It seemed Satan was hitting me in every avenue available- all the way from health crisis to financial difficulties to family struggles, and etc. Because none of these difficulties seemed to be working out, even though God had promised me an open door, I began to wonder if there was something wrong in my life. Was I doing all I should, or was there something I was missing? Maybe a sin I was hiding?

God's Word tells us that if we hide sin we will not prosper. I sure didn't seem to be prospering, so this really began to bother me. Many times I searched my life in the light of God's Word, trying to figure out why these matters were not being solved. This was troubling me so much that it became increasingly difficult to think of anything else. Finally, claiming Philippians 4:6-7, I left it with God. I asked Him to please give me peace in this matter and show me if there was anything wrong in my life.

A few days later, our church held a Bible conference. The first few days of this conference will be forever etched in my memory, because they were among my most miserable ever spent. First of all, God revealed just how rotten and unworthy I really was. He took me back to my right- eousness as a filthy rag. If you're willing to go all the way with God, you'll find in yourself there is no good.

I heard a song the other day which perfectly expressed just how worthy you and I honestly are. It proclaimed, "The only man made thing in heaven will be the nail prints in Jesus' hands." I felt so low-like crawling under the table. God spoke to my heart saying, "Whatever made you think you could ever be worthy of a single Good News Club or anything else?" That's where the teacher stopped and I spent a whole day in that miserable state. I knew God was speaking to me and it caused me to feel very weak.

Praise the Lord! The message the next night was, "God uses weak people." This is why Jesus died for us. It's out of our weakness that his strength is made perfect. I left the meeting that night literally glowing, because this message was also for me. The following evening God gave me complete peace in knowing my heart was right with Him and I was simply waiting for His time. That night's message was on waiting on the Lord. I had been willing to go all the way with God to discover any wrong in my life-no matter how much it hurt, and He graciously let me know that all was well between us. We were just waiting on Him.

Less than a week later we took Carrie to the hospital. Can you imagine the peace I find in knowing that she isn't laying there due to God's chastisement upon me? Thank God, He let me go through all those problems until I so desperately sought the peace of knowing I was right with Him before this happened.

CHAPTER 16

DON'T WORRY ABOUT CARRIE

"Don't worry about anything; instead, pray about everything; tell God your needs and don't forget to thank him for his answers. If you do this you will experience God's peace, which is far more wonderful than the human mind can understand. His peace will keep your thoughts and your hearts quiet and at rest as you trust in Christ Jesus" (Philippians 4:6-7-TLB).

Two of my favorite Bible verses are Philippians 4:6-7. They have become a real source of comfort through Carrie's illness. I find the center part of these verses a real test of the first part and the last. Do you have God's peace in whatever has been bothering you? If not, you're either worrying, haven't told God about it, or are not trusting Jesus in it.

The Lord taught me this in a very meaningful way earlier this year. I had just taken over as chairman of the Women's Missionary Union in our church. I definitely felt the Lord's leadership in accepting this position, although I knew very little about it. The very first month, just a couple of days after our first meeting, I discovered that we had an associational meeting in our church. This would include an all day meeting and lunch. As was my usual custom, I began to stew. Oh, I had memorized Philippians 4:6-7, but I hadn't paid much attention to applying them to my life, at least not enough.

One morning while washing dishes and stewing, I

protested, *"What a terrible time for this, right after Christmas, and I have already committed myself to some other things. Lord, I don't have time for this and I don't know how to go about it and . . ."*

Once again the Lord reminded me of those Philippians verses. I had forgotten most of them, so I took time to look them up and learn them again. *"Okay, Lord," I prayed. "I won't worry about it. I'll just pray about it and do what you show me."*

Although Satan tried very hard to shake me from this several times-such as the night before when the special music canceled and my phone was out of order so I couldn't call in another-I held to it and found it really works. Every detail worked out just beautifully. On the day of the meeting I was as calm as could be, actually even enjoyed it.

How I appreciate this lesson now. Worrying about a meeting is not even in the same ballpark as worrying when your daughter's blood sugar goes down to 0 and she stops breathing, or up to 800. How glad I was that God had taught me that He honestly meant what He said.

One day while sitting with Carrie I looked up, and much to my delight, I saw two good friends coming toward me. One of the ladies had met with me every week to pray for the Good News Clubs and had become quite dear. It's hard to pray so closely with a person and not learn to love them. At this particular time it was a delight to see her coming.

That day she shared an experience with me which later proved to be a real comfort. She testified, "When I first heard about Carrie, the Holy Spirit came over me a way I had never experienced before. I began to weep uncontrollably for her. After a while the Lord spoke to my heart and said, 'Don't worry about Carrie. I'm taking care of her. You pray for the family.'" Of course, this is the same thing He

says in his Word. How good it is to know that God promises to take care of us.

So many times we get so caught up in our troubles that
we forget this truth and can't see the blessings God is bringing us. If I were to sit here and count all night, I could not
begin to number the blessings He has bestowed through
Carrie's illness to others as well as to my family and me.
As for Carrie, I wonder if she isn't just lying in the Master's
arms. God certainly has promised that He is taking care of
her.

CHAPTER 17

JOY THROUGH TEARS

"The Lord is near unto those who are of a broken heart" (Psalm 34:18 KJV).

I spoke in earlier chapters of how I broke down and wept a couple of times while Carrie was in this coma. I believe both of these were wrong. The first was a lack of faith on my part, and the second was trying to face the future all at once.

Hold on a minute, I did not mean all tears are wrong. I had a fabulous experience one day while weeping. It was the eighteenth day Carrie was in the Bartlesville hospital and it had been a rough day physically. I was feeling miserable. The doctor told me earlier that morning that he wanted to do a brain scan on Carrie, which was to determine if there was a blood clot or any abnormalities. Two of my friends came to visit earlier that morning, and seeing it was a rough day had stayed on into the afternoon. It seemed as if it took forever to move Carrie into the room to do the test.

As we sat in the waiting room, a lady from the office brought us the bill. It was more than my husband's entire yearly salary for just eighteen days. That was extremely hard to swallow. One of my friends wisely suggested we go down to the chapel and pray about it. Back to Philippians 4:6-7. I decided to follow God's Word and not worry about it.

We had tried taking out insurance a few years pervious, only to discover they would not cover Carrie. Now, left without any means of paying this much money, I turned to God. "Father, you said not to worry about anything, to tell you our needs and you will meet them according to your riches in glory." This is a lot of money to me, and we'll probably need a lot more before this is over, but I know it's just a drop in the bucket for you. She's your child too, so we need this much and more. Thank you for supplying it and thank you for letting us trust you for it, in Jesus' name, Amen." I turned it over to Jesus and refused to worry about it again.

Soon afterwards Carrie was brought back to her room and my friends left so I could be with her. As I sat there waiting for the report, the tears began to flow. Every time I attempted to talk my voice would quiver and the weeping would begin again.

The Lord had blessed us with a Christian nurse that day. She walked over, wrapped her arms around me and said, "As much as I can, I know what you're going though. Can I help in any way? Can I call my pastor and ask him to come?"

"No, but thank you," I responded. I appreciated her concern but thought that perhaps if I didn't try to talk I would weather the storm. Not wanting to leave until the test results were completed, I waited silently while fighting back the tears.

As soon as the doctor came he informed me that the brain scan appeared to be fine. I immediately went outside to sit in the car; or rather, to water its inside. This time it wasn't a lack of faith or facing the whole future at once, it was simply exhaustion and human emotion. Never before had I felt the presence of the Lord any stronger than that day while sitting in my vehicle weeping. Doesn't the Bible tell us, "The Lord is near unto those who are of a broken heart"?

Sometime later I learned our pastor had become concerned because I seemed to be penning up my emotions and had called a special prayer chain about this. Do you suppose I wept while they prayed?

CHAPTER 18

A GLOW IN THE DARK

"They looked unto him, and were radiant, and their faces were not ashamed" (Psalm 34:5 KJV).

God, in all His wisdom, picked out each and every verse to be written in the Bible, and one of the most beautiful must be Psalm 34:5. During Carrie's illness, I learned the true meaning of this verse. I found that if you seek the Lord, if you look unto Him, your face will be radiant, aglow with His love and peace, until others will see this in you. In fact, they may tend to wonder if you might not be just a little crazy.

God can turn the darkest day into one of joy and light. Carrie seemed to be doing just fine. She was still in a coma, but appeared to be improving. She was relaxing more, opening her eyes, and occasionally following someone with them. She even seemed to recognize our voices. She was off all the machines now and we truly believed she was improving.

Upon arriving at the hospital this particular day, I found her seemingly where she'd been weeks earlier. Her breathing was extremely heavy and she was once again tense. When I tried talking to her, she didn't appear to know I was present. Once again the tears began to flow. Turning to the window so no one would see me, I fought to hold them back.

"Lord," I whispered, "this is a terrible witness. Please help me to stop." Then I remembered what I had told

Charles the Sunday before: "I believe the Lord is so in charge here, He is even over my tears. If I had not cried at times, perhaps people would think I just didn't care. Perhaps they wouldn't have realized the Lord was giving me the power to get through this with a smile."

Now I stopped and gave the rest of the day over to Him, "Whether for joy or tears, Lord, you take over." Immediately after voicing this prayer I remembered what He had taught me about taking one day at a time. Again I prayed and asked Him to give me grace enough to walk through this one day. As I turned around and looked back at Carrie, the tears once again began to flow.

The Lord quickly reminded me of another truth, ". . . in everything give thanks," so I began giving thanks. I've heard many people say, "I may be able to give thanks in a situation, but certainly not for it." I've never understood this. To me it's like splitting hairs. In Psalm 37:23 we are told, "The steps of a good man are ordered by the Lord and He delights in his way." If God has ordered this day for me, then why can't I give thanks for everything?

I was well into the process of giving thanks for everything when in walked three young people from a church in Bartlesville. They had visited us before. It was apparent that one of them was an individual who lived by sight. As far as he was concerned, Carrie was better only if it showed. He would always ask if there were any signs of improvement and desired to hear what the doctor's report had said. This troubled me after his last visit and I later wished I had challenged his concept of belief only by sight.

Now today he began this same old pattern, so I answered his questions and then added, "I'm sure at least most of the doctors would give her little hope, but as Christians we do not walk by sight but by faith."

Not only did this encourage these young people-they began praising the Lord-but after sharing some Scripture with them, I had talked myself out of this slump and was again walking by faith instead of sight. The rest of this day was indescribable. It quickly became one of the best in my life. The Lord completely took over and I found a quiet peace and great joy!

It seemed as though people flocked into Carrie's room, furnishing me with several opportunities to witness for the Lord. There was no doubt that all who ventured in received a blessing. One lady who visited and brought me a Christian book later confessed to a friend of mine, "I don't know why I took her that book. She is literally glowing."

"They looked unto him and were radiant."

CHAPTER 19

THROUGH THE STORM

"For He shall give his angels charge over thee, to keep thee in all thy ways" (Psalm 91:11 KJV).

While driving home from Bartlesville one day, I noticed some very ominous looking clouds ahead. In just a few minutes, I would be entering into an extremely dangerous thunderstorm. A smile surfaced on my face as I remember back to another heavy rainstorm that had threatened me only weeks earlier. The rain fell so hard the road wasn't even visible. This prevented me from pulling over to the side, because I couldn't see what I would be pulling onto. This was a dangerous situation and I had no choice but to continue driving at a slow rate of speed. Since the center line in the highway was visible, I simply followed it.

Meanwhile, I began to pray. "Heavenly Father, I need one of your angels to help me drive. I can't see the road and you've promised to keep me. Or if you would rather, you could just stop the rain." The rain stopped immediately! No doubt I was quite surprised, but I continued on my way praising Him.

Several times since then I have faced bad weather, but never with fear. Now, while looking at these new and threatening clouds, I softly thanked Him for taking care of me and continued singing, "When the Roll is Called up Yonder, I'll be there." Still unable to get my mind completely off the rain, I soon found myself singing, "When the Rain is Called up Yonder, I'll be there."

How marvelous God is! How He cares for His children is above and beyond what we can comprehend. About two minutes before reaching Independence the rain began, although the Lord did hold back the worst of the storm until I was safely home. This thunderous down-pour continued for over two hours. How grateful I was for deciding to return home early that evening.

Perhaps if I had moaned and complained, I might not have arrived home before the storm began. The children of Israel turned an eleven day trip into forty years, moaning and complaining all the way. If we put our trust in God, I believe it delights Him to work things out for us.

CHAPTER 20

CHILD OF THE KING

"But as many as received him, to them gave He power to become children of God, even to them that believe on his name" (John 1:12 KJV).

One day while sitting by Carrie's bedside I looked up to see three ladies standing by the door gazing into our room. Since I didn't recognize them, this was a little surprising. I silently prayed that God would show me what to say.

One of the ladies asked, "Is she any better?"

"I think she's about the same," I replied.

Then another one questioned, "How old is she?"

"Fifteen," I answered.

As they turned and walked away, the third lady whispered, "Tsk! Tsk! Poor little thing."

I didn't think quickly enough to respond to her remark. As I turned and walked back toward Carrie it hit me, and speaking out loud I said, "Poor little thing! You are not a poor little thing! You're a child of the King. In fact, you are a child of the King of kings and Lord of lords."

I looked down at Carrie and saw that she was smiling. It was a very quick smile, and yet it was there. To my knowledge, this was the only time she had smiled since she went into this coma.

I knew I shouldn't just drop it there with these ladies, so I watched for them to pass by again. When they did, guess what I did? You're right again. Nothing! "Lord, I should have said something, shouldn't I?" I whispered. He reminded me of the scripture where Paul stated, "I will talk about Jesus to all who will listen." I knew I should have said something, so stating, "All right Lord, you do this," I hurried to the door and called them back.

"I'd like to share something with you," I spoke. Then I shared what I had said and how Carrie had smiled and added, "She is far better off right now than most people will ever be." I went on to explain that she is a Christian and in God's hands. They stood there, in shock I suppose, saying very little. I had spoken in much fear and trembling, and yet I am sure they saw my sincerity and I have no doubt it made a lasting impression on them.

Looking back now, I wish I had said more. If only I had thought to ask, "Are you ready?" and then gone on to share the gospel and an invitation to receive Christ. How many times and how sadly I've failed the Lord. Even so, He is working on me, teaching, training, and helping. At least the seeds were planted in those ladies' hearts that day. Then again, maybe that's what God wanted. I had prayed, "Lord, You do this." He could have urged me on.

The truth I'm trying to express is that you should not be afraid to try because you might say something wrong. It is the Holy Spirit who convicts, and He can use your weakest words. The only condition you must meet is being willing and ready.

The Bible tells us what we must do to be ready. "Study to show thyself approved unto God, a workman that need not to be ashamed, rightly dividing the word of truth" (2 Timothy 2:15). How can you speak for God if you haven't been in his Word enough to know what He says? If you're willing to study, pray, and follow his leading, He will do the rest.

CHAPTER 21

I CAN'T HOLD ON

*"To his own master he stands or falls. Yea, he shall
be held up. For God is able to make him stand"*
(Romans 14:4 KJV).

God has promised to meet our needs. I feel one of my
needs is to be home with my family, and God had just
convinced me of this at the time Carrie's illness began. Yet
now it was impossible because I also needed to be with her.
So what should I do? It seems I'm stuck.

I took this need to God in prayer and He met it, but not
in the way I had hoped. He didn't heal Carrie so I could take
her home; instead, He met it by having a relative offer to
keep the kids for three weeks. Although I was thankful for
this, it was only a temporary solution. I knew when they
returned home the problem would again be there.

Because of this, and other reasons, I thought Carrie
would at least be improved to where I wouldn't need to
spend as much time at the hospital when my other children
returned. Well, it didn't happen that way. When they
returned home, she was still just holding her own. I felt
God had let me down, even broken a promise. It was at this
discouraging point that I began to question my faith, if God
didn't mean this promise, then what about the rest? Is any
of this real?

How could I fall this low after all God had done for me?
I can't describe the horror of thinking maybe this is all my
imagination. Maybe it isn't real after all. But even as I

questioned God, there was the deep cry in my heart, *Please God! Don't let me turn back.* As I felt all faith fading, I remembered God was able to hold on to me. "My sheep hear my voice, and I know them, and they follow me. I give unto them eternal life; and they shall never perish; neither shall any man pluck them out of my hand. My Father, who gave them to me, is greater than all, and no man is able to pluck them out of My hand" (John 10:27-29 KJV). I prayed, "Please, Lord, I can't hold on to you. You hold on to me." After this, I relaxed and quit worrying.

I felt very empty the rest of that day, but I refused to think about it. When I awoke the next morning, God began working on my thoughts. I don't remember the scripture He used or how He did it, but He faithfully held on and lifted me out of my despair.

Although this was one of the hardest lessons of my life, perhaps it was also one of the most important. Which of us could hang on for ourselves? What joy it brings to know I don't have to hang on, God will. Our faith might fail, but we "live by the faith of the Son of God" (Galatians 2:20 KJV). His faith will never fail! Praise God! Once we come to Him, He is able to make us stand!

A couple of days after this, a friend went to Bartlesville with me. I had already decided that my doubt of God's existence was one experience I would not share with anyone. As far as I was concerned it was too horrible to be revealed. Yet as we drove along visiting that day, I was amazed to hear her sharing how she also once had an experience just like mine. She couldn't have known about mine, for I had not shared it with anyone, yet here she was telling me of an identical experience in her own life.

I remembered where Paul wrote, "There is no temptation taken you but such as is common to man." I realized that

God had just proven this to me. Other Christians go through similar experiences as we do, but it is not God who tempts us, we are all tempted when we are drawn away by our own lust.

Then God reminded me of another principle of His. In a devotion I had once read, a certain man had one particular sin he kept committing. He would go to the Lord, confess it, turn from it, but sooner or later he would do it again. One day, after once more committing that particular sin, he went to the Lord and confessed, "Well, Lord, I've done it again." The Lord answered, "Done what again?"

How true this is. Although sin always causes problems, as well as loss of blessings, still this is a correct statement. God promises to forget our sin, to remember it no more. Once it's confessed, not only does He forgive and cleanse us, He also forgets it. I knew God had forgotten all about my lack of faith, and as an added blessing, I was able to build up a Christian friend by sharing this with her when she was really down.

Looking back at events such as this, I stand in awe at the way God brings us through each of the difficulties we face, using these situations as bread for us to grow on. It's wonderful how He brings each one of us in contact with the right person at the right time. One event leads to another, and finally all fit together to make a perfect plan.

I believe it will be awesome when we arrive in heaven and can then look back to see the total picture. No wonder Paul could say, "Who will free me from my slavery to this deadly lower nature? Thank God! It has been done by Jesus Christ our Lord. He has set me free" (Romans 7:25: TLB).

CHAPTER 22

MY WORK FINISHED

"Say not ye, There are yet four months, and then cometh harvest? Behold, I say unto you, Lift up your eyes, and look on the fields; for they are white already to harvest" (John 4:35; KJV).

One Sunday morning as I was sitting in church, the Lord spoke to me through the responsive reading, John 4:35. I found myself thinking back through each step of this ordeal with Carrie. First, I had been willing to go any direction God wanted with her; therefore I had sought His will so I could pray accordingly. When I felt He had revealed it to me, I agreed with it, claimed it, and walked in it-literally sending out my singers (2 Chronicles 20). I praised the Lord for healing both in my heart and to the public.

After that, I sought God's will daily. Now as I read back over that scripture, God let me know that I had done all He asked and now my work with Carrie was finished. I was to look on for what He had for me next. I prayed God would show me what to do, where my part was in the harvest.

As we prepared lunch that afternoon, my daughters and I were singing the song printed in the front of this book. Later, after leaving home to drive back to Bartlesville, the chorus kept running through my mind, "Lift it high in the sky, let the whole world know." The Lord had already shown me that the world was the limit. He had taught me a truth and I was to share it with my generation. He had given me an open door. Now I felt He was leading to go and share it. "How Lord? How can I in a hospital room?" Of course! Write it down. Write a book! "Lord, I can't do that, but I know you can."

CHAPTER 23

WHEN FEAR CREPT IN

"When I am afraid I will trust in thee" (Psalm 56:3 KJV).

It was Tuesday, August 5th, and Carrie had been in the coma 98 days. Her temperature had risen to 104, her blood sugar was up, and her breathing wasn't right. It was erratic and fast for a while, and then would almost stop. The doctor told us her brain was not working well enough to control her respiratory system.

She had continually worsened throughout the day, so I decided to spend the night with her. When Charles called, I told him Carrie had worsened and he came to the hospital. That night about four o'clock she was very near death's door. She couldn't get enough air and it appeared as though she was drowning. I believed the hospital personnel believed she was dying so they just left us alone with her. Finally, I couldn't take it any longer and cried out, "Oh God! Please take her. Please don't let her suffer any longer." I had just finished speaking this when God checked me and I thought, *"Oh no! That wasn't what you told me to pray. I'm sorry. I take it back, but Lord, I don't have faith to hold up under these circumstances."* He reminded me of Galatians 2:20. It was not my faith I had to go on, it was His.

I prayed, "Okay, Lord. Give me your faith; but Lord, a Christian, whether dying or not should not have to go through this kind of fear. Please give her peace." In a matter of minutes she was breathing normal, her fever was breaking, and she was asleep. She rested this way for several days.

One of the fascinating things about this experience was the way the Lord had prepared me for it. That day, a certain person that I had come into contact with several times throughout Carrie's illness decided I needed counseling. Although he had asked me about her a few times and offered to help, that was the extent of our conversations. Strange that this was to be the day he decided I needed counseling. He asked me how I felt. I answered, "Fine. I believe the Lord is in charge."

"No," he protested. "That is not what I mean. How do you feel, not what do you think?"

"I don't understand," I questioned. "How do I separate how I feel and what I think?"

Then he added, "I mean in your stomach." He proceeded to tell me that some people believe fear to be a sin, but it wasn't.

"Well," I replied, "I know fear is a human emotion and will creep in, but it seems to me if you hang on to it, then it becomes sin." David said, "When I am afraid I will trust the Lord."

He became somewhat frustrated with me and finally gave up. That night I knew why God had sent him my way. Many times, as I felt fear creeping in, I remembered that verse and what I had said to him, and then I turned it back over to the Lord. Now, as it appeared as though Carrie was dying, I not only found great comfort in this, but also found courage to sit on her bed and comfort her. I desperately desired to turn away, for it was extremely difficult to see her this way. But as I turned my fear over to Jesus, I decided that if she was going to die, it wasn't going to be alone. I was going to hold her hand until Jesus took it.

CHAPTER 24

HIDDEN IN MY HEART

"And he went down with them, and came to Nazareth, and was subject to them; but his mother kept all these sayings in her heart." (Luke 2:51 KJV).

God makes us, like Mary, many promises. As Christians, we have a book of promises called the Bible. As we study and pray and God molds our lives around his Word, these become personal promises to us. Perhaps this is one of the reasons it is called the "Living Word." Not only does it bring eternal life as we believe, but it also lives for each of us individually. I have many of his promises hidden in my heart.

All through Carrie's illness and before, I believe God had promised healing. He had promised this in many ways. The first was about one and one-half years ago when I was listening to some Jack Taylor tapes. These were tremendous tapes dealing with finding the will of God, agreeing with it, and praying the Scripture. This was partly new to me and I found it fascinating. God was blessing me greatly. As I studied and applied these principles, I found my prayer time so exciting I could hardly contain myself. I was getting up at 5 a.m. to have an hour alone with God, and even that didn't seem like nearly long enough.

During this time, we were having a series of meetings in our church. I was also working with the Good News Clubs and was very busy. Carrie's disease had become difficult because a diabetic must have certain foods at certain times.

I had stopped to prepare her meal, and as I worked, I prayed, "Lord, this diabetes is such a problem. I don't have time for it. It's so hard on Carrie, especially as a teen. You could heal her if you wanted to." I could almost hear Him respond, "Yes, I could." That shook me, and I realized it was up to me to find out if this was His will. As I prayed and studied the scriptures, I became convinced that this was what God wanted. I prayed for healing, thanked Him for it, and left it there. Once in a while, I would remember this promise and thank Him again for healing her.

Last winter, we were again having another series of meetings and the same problems with Carrie's special meals arose. I reminded God of His promise to heal her, "Lord, I'm not trying to rush you or anything, but I believe You have promised to heal her." It was a short time later that Carrie became ill with the flu. Somehow it acted against her diabetes and she ended up in the hospital in a coma. She came out of that first coma, but from then on she had problems. Every time we would think we had it under control and her blood sugar was staying where it should, another difficulty would arise and she would once again get sick.

Even though Carrie's diabetes had been under control for almost four years, in the last few months she had been sick several times. After the third time she was sick, I had sat up with her a couple of nights and was exhausted and scared. When she was past the crisis and just resting, I went downstairs and picked up my Bible. As I opened my Bible, I whispered, "Lord, I don't know, just give me whatever you have for me. I could sure use some encouragement."

At first, as I read, it didn't seem to mean a lot. The portion I was reading was to the children of Israel, but then I came to a verse I couldn't get away from. There isn't any other way to explain it, other than I kept reading, but it kept pulling me back. No matter what I was reading, that verse kept going through my mind. *"No,"* I thought, *"That verse was written to Israel. It couldn't apply to me, or could it?"* The verse surely fit the occasion. It said, "There will be a night of terror and then the healing." Could it apply to the children of Israel and to me? God seemed to be trying to show me something through it.

I thought maybe she was going to have a crisis that night and then get better, but she didn't. She just gradually improved, so I forgot about the verse. After Carrie went into this coma and became critical, I remembered that verse. I can't think of a better way to describe this than a night of terror.

Since then, I believe God has continually led us in many different ways to pray for healing. Almost every time I opened my Bible, no matter what part I was studying, the same message came through. "Trust me for healing, wait patiently for me and I will heal her." Many others believed this also, and there was a presence of God in Carrie's room which many have commented on.

One day while I was standing by Carrie's bed, I remembered someone in the Bible saying, "Jesus, if you will, you can heal her." I repeated this same statement to Him. Then the answer came in my mind just as clearly as if Jesus had been standing beside me. "Yes," I heard, "I will." The presence of His Holy Spirit suddenly flooded my being. I could give many more examples of this because every time we started to doubt, He would again send reassurance. He would take us back to the Scripture and give us His assurance that healing was what He wanted.

As the days passed, it became very hard to continue trusting Him for healing when she was so desperately sick, and Satan continually worked on us. God taught us that Satan will fight us, when we are close to his jugular vein. I knew that when Carrie came out of this, God would be glorified in a mighty way and Satan didn't like it.

The date was August 20, 1975. The time was 4:45 a.m. God answered our prayer! Carrie went to be with Him. This probably would have shaken me, but again, He had us totally prepared. A couple of days earlier Carrie's condition was once again growing worse. Much of her hair was falling out and she seemed to be in so much pain. Each time they moved her she would moan for several minutes in pain.

It was at this time, while reading in Hebrews, that I came to this scripture, "These all died in faith, not having received the promises but having seen them afar off, and were persuaded of them, and embraced them, and confessed that they were strangers and pilgrims on the earth. For they that say such things declare plainly that they seek a country. And if they had been mindful of that country from which they came out, they might have had opportunity to return. But now they desire a better country, that is, an heavenly; wherefore, God is not ashamed to be called their God; for He hath prepared for them a city" (Hebrews 11:13-16 KJV). I have wondered many times if the Lord showed Carrie a glimpse of heaven and she didn't want to come back.

Also, it had come to the place where Charles and I felt so badly about leaving the rest of the family so much that we were really praying God would end this as soon as possible. My prayer had been that He would end it by the time school started.

Carrie seemed to be in so much pain that we could no longer pray in our hearts for God to keep her on this earth. Although we were still praying for healing, in my heart, I couldn't ask her to live another day.

I went home the morning after her death and picked up my Bible. *"Lord, I don't really understand what happened,"* I prayed, *"but I'll take whatever you want to give me. Whether it's understanding or just believing you know what you're doing."*

My Bible fell open to Psalm 111 (KJV)and I read these words, "He will ever be mindful of his covenant . . . He has shown His people the power of His works . . . all His commandments are sure . . . the fear of the Lord is the beginning of wisdom . . . a good understanding have all they that do His commandments." I knew some day I would understand why He had led us to pray for healing when He knew that Carrie was going to die.

There were times I had doubts. Did we give up too soon? If we had continued to pray for healing with our hearts, would she have lived? Did God really lead us to pray for healing, or had we misunderstood Him? One of the most wonderful aspects about this whole experience is the way God loved us through this time of grief, even when doubt crept in. God understood how deep the hurt was and how much I wanted to please Him. He did not scold or punish. He just let me cry it out, and He even blessed while I did.

In the weeks to follow, God kept taking me back to that scripture in Hebrews. "These all died in faith, not having received the promises but having seen them afar off . . ." Then He took me to another scripture, "By faith in the name of Jesus, this man whom you see and know was made strong. It is Jesus' name and the faith that comes through Him that has given this complete healing to him, as you can all see" (Acts 3:16-NIV).

Finally, I began to understand. Yes, God had led us to pray for healing; and yes, I believe He had promised to heal her. God taught me that even though we may not see the answers to His promises, it doesn't mean He didn't keep them. While I didn't see Carrie rise up and walk out of the hospital, she did. She was totally healed. We may not see all the results of God's promises until we reach that city whose maker and builder is God. But be assured, He will keep each one.

I'd like to share a truth with you which God has made very meaningful to me. If my family and I were all being tortured in prison and one of us escaped, there isn't any way I could wish that one back because the rest of us missed them. Yet that is what death is for the Christian, being let out of this prison body, being set free! Yes, we miss Carrie. We miss her terribly. There is an empty spot in our hearts, but there is also joy in knowing she is with Jesus and some-day we will be with her again.

From the time I became a Christian, I have been stacking up treasure in heaven. The Bible says, "Where your treasure is, there will your heart be also." A greater part of my heart is in heaven today-one of my most precious treasures is there.

Thank God she was ready!!!

Now I want to ask you a question. Please consider this carefully. If you woke up to discover your life on this earth over, would you be ready to meet God? Surely one of the saddest words that will be spoken by the lost throughout all eternity will be "almost." King Agrippa said to Paul, "Almost thou persuaded me to be a Christian" (Acts 26:28 KJV). But almost isn't good enough! Almost is to fail. You will be failing both you and your family. Don't fail. If you're not ready to meet Jesus, you need to make this deci-sion now. God's Word tells us how. John 3:16 (KJV) reads, "For God so loved the world, that He gave His only begotten Son, that whosoever believeth in Him should not perish, but have everlasting life." That "whosoever" means you. God loves you!

God's Word also tells us that all have sinned. You have and I have. One of the best definitions of sin I have found is in 1 John 5:17 (KJV). "All unrighteousness is sin." Unrighteousness is anything that is not right. Put simply, sin is the wrong things we think, say, or do, and sometimes the things we don't do that we should. Sin separates us from a Holy God, and we cannot go to heaven because of this sin. But the Lord Jesus Christ, God's perfect Son, God Himself, gave His blood for your sin so you could be forgiven. He took your punishment when He died on the cross. 1 John 1:7 (KJV) reads, ". . . the blood of Jesus Christ, his Son cleanses us from all sin." As we find in 1 Corinthians 15:3-4 (KJV), He died for our sin, was buried, and rose again the third day. Also, John 1:12 (KJV) reads, "But as many as received him, to them gave He power to become children of God, even to them that believe on His name." Will you believe in Him and receive Him as your Savior? I like to explain the word "receive" with Revelation 3:20 (KJV): "Behold, I stand at the door and knock; if any man hear My voice, and open the door, I will come into him, and will sup with him, and he with Me." Jesus is standing at the door of your heart (not the blood pumping organ, but the part of you that's really you) asking to be let in. Will you open the door and let Him in?

If so, pray this prayer:

"Dear Lord Jesus, I realize I have sinned. I believe you died for my sins, gave your blood so I could be forgiven, were buried and rose again. I want to turn from my sin. I invite you into my heart. I trust you as my Savior and I want to follow you as my Lord. Thank you for forgiving and saving me. Amen."

If you prayed this prayer and meant it in your heart, then God promised to send His Holy Spirit to dwell inside of you. Also, He has promised, "I will never leave thee, nor forsake thee" (Hebrews 13:5 KJV). 1 John 5:12 (KJV) tells us, "He that hath the Son hath life." This is present tense. It doesn't mean sometime in the future you may have it, it means you have it right now through forever. While your body will die because of sin (unless Jesus returns first), the part of you that's really you will live with Jesus forever! Praise the Lord! He's with you now and forever.

Now, if you're not already, you need to begin attending a good Bible believing church. God has also said, "Whosoever, therefore, shall confess me before men, him will I confess also before My Father, who is in heaven. But whosoever shall deny me before men, him will I also deny before My Father, who is in heaven" (Matthew 10:32-33 KJV).

You should also study the Bible regularly and practice what God says. Now that you are a Christian, when you sin, you need to confess it to God. 1 John 1:9 (KJV) assures us, "If we confess our sins, He is faithful and just to forgive us our sins, and to cleanse us from all unrighteousness."

When you sin and do not confess it you don't lose your salvation, but you will lose your fellowship, your joy, and your peace with God. King David had a man murdered and committed adultery with his wife, yet he had not lost his salvation. Yes, he had lost his joy, but not his salvation. He prayed, ". . . restore unto me the joy of thy salvation" (Psalm 51:12 KJV). David did not pray restore unto me my salvation; He prayed restore unto me the joy of my salvation.

You will also need to spend time in prayer each day,

which is a very important part of Christian growth; and as you grow as a Christian, you should begin sharing your faith by telling others what Jesus has done for you.

Another act of obedience for a believer is tithing-giving at least one-tenth of your income to God. By doing this you will be freeing God to "supply all your needs" as we find in Philippians 4:19.

As you do these things, you will grow as a Christian and continue in peace and happiness.

One of the first verses you need to learn is, "I am crucified with Christ; nevertheless I live; yet not I, but Christ lives in me; and the life which I now live in the flesh I life by the faith of the Son of God, who loved me and gave Himself for me" (Galatians 2:20 KJV). This verse teaches us that Jesus is living out His life through us. It is He who makes us able to live victoriously. As we yield our lives to Him and trust Him, He will give us the victory.

CHAPTER 25

JOY COMETH IN THE MORNING

"Weeping may endure for a night, but joy cometh in the morning" (Psalm 30:5 KJV).

What a beautiful day! It is March, almost a year since the beginning of this story. Rain has been gently falling most of the day, and it's so cold that it's freezing on the bushes and trees, coating them with a layer of ice. As I gaze out the window, it reminds me of a winter wonderland, except for the spots of green in the grass that indicate spring is just around the corner.

On a day like this, I feel like David when he said, "What is man that Thou art mindful of him?" What a wonderful God we have, a God who cares so much about each of us! If He can give us a beautiful day like this on this earth, just think what wonders He must have in store for us in heaven.

It's exciting to think about heaven, because just like spring, Christ's coming back for His own must be right around the corner, even at the doors. Yet while it's an exciting time, it's also a troubled time. I continue to think about those who would not be ready if He came today. There will be many families broken up, not just for a short time as mine was, but for all eternity. How sad it makes me to consider how many children are lost-many of them the children of Christian parents. How many parents are so busy, "working their fingers to the bone," to give their children the things this world has to offer, yet neglect to give them that which really counts-Jesus? What if we give them all that

94

this world has to offer, but they're lost for all eternity? How important are the things we gave our children for these few short years on earth going to be?

God gave us the means and the instructions to bring our children in. Some parents feel that if they take them to Sunday school, or even go with them, they have fulfilled their duty. Yes, that is a good beginning, but it isn't enough. PARENTS, you are responsible for the salvation of your own children! You can bring them in. That is the message God taught me and told me to give to my generation. I believe as Mr. Overholtzer, founder of Child Evangelism Fellowship, believed over seventy years ago: if each Christian parent would find out how and lead each one of their own children to Christ at the age God commanded, I believe every one of them would be saved. If you didn't reach your children at this age, don't give up, read on. You must be willing to pay the cost. It will mean total commitment on your part. Let's see what the Scripture has to say about this.

First, let's look at Eli (1 Samuel 2 & 3). He was a priest of the Lord, yet his heart was not right with God. He was not bringing up his sons in the way they should go. Look at what God said to Eli, ". . . the iniquity of Eli's house shall not be purged with sacrifice nor offering forever . . ." (1 Samuel 3:14 KJV). They were lost for all eternity because he was not bringing them up as God commanded.

Now let's consider Noah, a just man who walked with God. When God looked down and saw how evil the people on his earth had become, He was sorry He had even made them. He decided He was going to destroy mankind from off the face of the earth with a flood. However, here was this one just man. God told Noah to build an ark, and Noah obeyed. Do you know what God said to Noah? "Come into the ark, you and your whole family . . ." (Genesis 7:1 NIV). Jesus is our ark of safety today, and God gives each of us the same invitation. "Come into the ark, you and your whole family."

Joshua said, "Choose you this day whom ye will serve . . . but as for me and my house, we will serve the Lord" (Joshua 24:15 KJV). Do you see what he was saying? He was not saying, "I'm going to let my children grow up and then, when they are old enough, they can decide for themselves what they want to believe." He was confessing, "I have the authority over them."

I realize receiving Christ is an individual decision everyone must make for themselves, no one rides to heaven on the coat-tail of another. However, God put us together in families. If God could say, "Believe on the Lord Jesus Christ and thou shalt be saved and thy house" (Acts 16:31 KJV), I believe Him! We believe the first part of that verse is for us, why don't we believe the last part?

I believe we not only have the right, but in fact, a responsibility to reach our own families for Christ. The Bible tells us to, "Train up a child in the way he should go and when he is old he will not depart from it" (Proverbs 22:6 KJV). It also commands, "And, ye fathers, provoke not your children to wrath, but bring them up in the nurture and admonition of the Lord" (Ephesians 6:4: KJV).

Yet in 1 Corinthians 2:14 (KJV), we are told, "But the natural man receiveth not the things of the Spirit of God; for they are foolishness unto him, neither can he know them, because they are spiritually discerned." A child, as well as an adult, must be born again before he or she can understand the things of God.

Putting these scriptures together, we discover that we cannot "train up a child in the way he should go" unless he is a Christian, because he can't understand what you are saying. Also, without Christ in their life, they won't have the power to have victory over sin. Therefore, if we are to obey God and bring our children up in the way they should go, we must first lead them to Christ. God instructs every Christian parent to do this. I realize some people are teaching Proverbs 22:6 is not a promise but a probability, however, it does not make any difference which one it is, a promise or probability. You cannot train your children up in the way they should go unless you first lead them to Christ. Remember, before your child comes to Christ they can't understand what you're saying, they do not have power over sin, and instead are servants to sin (Romans 6:17-18).

If any of your children have not been saved and you want to bring them in, ask God for power to do it. Ask Him to teach you what you need to know; however, if you have not received Christ yourself, this is the first step. But if you have accepted Christ as your own Lord and Savior, you must make sure your sin account is up to date with Him. There is only one thing that defeats a Christian, and that is SIN.

Would you be willing to ask God to show you if there is anything in your life that is keeping your family and others from coming to Him? God may have to take you back in years and set you back on the right path where you took off on the wrong. You may have to correct an injury which you caused to come upon another person, or perhaps you need to forgive someone who has wronged you. You must be willing to do all He asks.

All four of my girls were saved within a year of the time I came to Christ. I don't remember knowing a lot about living in Christ, or a deeper walk with Him, or any such thing at the time. I was a brand new Christian. All I desired was

His will. He was everything to me. He was my life, and I so wanted my family to glorify Him.

God must have this place in your life. He must be this important to you. To fall short of this is sin, and He said, "If I regard iniquity in my heart the Lord will not hear me" (Psalm 66:18 KJV).

If God does not have first place in your life, please yield to Him right now. Ask Him to take over in your life and trust Him to do so. You must be willing to spend time in the Word with Him, because it will be through God's Word that He will teach you.

If you are still holding back, keep this in mind: there can't be any "fence straddling" on this one. You are either right with God and bringing your family and others in, or you are not and are driving them farther away. This is not fun and games were talking about, it is the difference between heaven and hell for both your family and others. Keep in mind that once you have placed God first in your life, confessed all the sin He has shown you, and He has forgiven your sin (1 John 1:9), this makes you right with God and places you on praying ground.

Prayer is the next step in bringing your family into God's family. Pray for them! Pray like you have never prayed before. Hang on to God for their salvation and ask Him to make them being lost a matter of your need. After I received Christ, I realized I had not brought my children up in the way they should go. If there had been any way to have gone back and raised them in Jesus, I would have done so, but there wasn't. So I begged God to give me another chance, to give back the years the locust had eaten, the wasted time, to save my children. I asked Him not to punish them for my sin. Their salvation became a desperate need of mine.

As I mentioned before, they were all saved within a year. If we could only understand the power of prayer! If you and I could see what happens when the most seemingly insignificant Christian takes their place in Jesus, and through the authority of His name starts praying for the lost, it would scare us. God gives us certain conditions of prevailing prayer. If we follow these we have what we ask. For these conditions see: Psalm 66:18; Mark 11:25; 1 John 3:22; 1 John 5:14; Matthew 21:22; Romans 10:17; Numbers 14:28; John 14:13-14; James 5:16; Luke 18:1-8; Romans 8:26-27; and 2 Corinthians 10:4-5.

Ask God to show you the strongholds though which Satan is keeping your family and others in bondage. As your heart lines up with the Word, then and only then can you begin praying down these strongholds. You can begin "bringing into captivity every thought to the obedience of Christ." There will not be much left for them to do but receive Christ as their Savior.

In the Jack Taylor tapes I mentioned in chapter 24, he brings this out. He teaches this truth: "An evangelism that does not recognize the lost are lost because they are supernaturally bound and blinded by Satan, and that it is going to take a supernatural work to free them, the work of praying them free, is a weak evangelism indeed." Pray much for them.

I want to emphasize one of the truths about prayer here. You must believe God. Believe you have His promise to save your family and claim their salvation. My son was saved about two minutes after I said, "I'm not going to accept Satan's doubts, Lord. You have promised me his salvation."

For those of you who have not trained up your children in the way they should go, there may still be time. God is no respecter of persons (Romans 2:11). He does not love me any more than He does you. If He gave me back the wasted years and saved my children, why wouldn't He do it for you?

Also, if some of you may not be able to get the time back because you have children who have already died, all you can do is leave it with God. While you may not be able to get the time back, neither can you be sure they weren't saved. The thief on the cross made a last minute decision and Jesus said, "Today shalt thou be with me in paradise" (Luke 23:43 KJV).

Step number three in bringing you family is in to tell them how. Don't ever assume because they see Christ in you, see you going to Sunday school and church, see you studying your Bible and in prayer, see you serving and reaching others, that they know how to get God into their life. I didn't! Yes, they should see these things or they probably won't listen anyway, but they need to be told how. The Bible says, "Faith cometh by hearing and hearing by the Word of God" (Romans 10:17 KJV).

There are only a few things a person must know before they can receive Christ:

1) God loves me (John 3:16).
2) I have sinned (Romans 3:23 & 6:23).
3) The Lord Jesus Christ, God's perfect Son, paid the price for my sin by dying on the cross for me, shedding His blood so I could be forgiven, was buried, rose again, and is living today (1 Corinthians 15:3-4; 1 John 1:7; Romans 5:8).
4) In order to be saved I must receive Him as my Savior and Lord (John 1:12 & Revelation 3:20).
5) I am saved (Hebrews 13:5 & John 3:36).

If you don't have the kind of family you can read the

Bible to, then work these in with your everyday conversation, such as, "Isn't it wonderful God loves us so much to give us a beautiful day like today?" Be sure they understand each of these five steps! Seek every opportunity to work these in as the Holy Spirit leads, and trust Him to convict and give them understanding.

MAKE SURE YOUR FAMILY IS IN!

CHAPTER 26

LET NOT THE APPLE OF THINE EYE CEASE

". . . Let tears run down like a river day and night; give thyself no rest; let not the apple of thine eye cease. Arise, cry out in the night; in the beginning of the watches pour out thine heart like water before the face of the Lord; lift up thy hands toward Him for the life of thy young children, who faint for hunger in the top of every street" (Lamentations 2:18-19 KJV).

If all your children are in, PRAISE GOD! What about those children around you whose parents are not bringing them to Christ? Don't they become our responsibility? Jesus said, ". . . it is not the will of your Father, who is in heaven, that one of these little ones should perish" (Matthew 18:14 KJV).

The scripture on the top of this page was written to Israel. They didn't listen, and their children were lost. Please read it again: ". . . Let tears run down like a river day and night; give thyself no rest; let not the apple of thine eye cease. Arise, cry out in the night; in the beginning of the watches pour out thine heart like water before the face of the Lord; lift up thy hands toward Him for the life of thy young children, who faint for hunger in the top of every street." Our children are seeking so desperately to find the meaning of life that in many cases before they turn ten, eleven, or twelve years of age, they have turned to sex, alcohol, drugs, Satan worship, and sins of every kind. Children will follow any leader who teaches them, whether the teaching is true or false.

If our nation is going to survive, we must teach our children God's way and reach them for Christ. We are often so quick to criticize and point out when we see children misbehaving, and then talk about how terrible this generation is, but I don't believe we have a right to criticize unless we are willing to make every effort to reach them and teach them the right way first. Some will listen.

Also, it is important to reach them at as young of an age as possible. I'd like to share a favorite poem with you. Please read it carefully!

THE BENT TWIG
It hurt my heart to see today
Someone with whom I used to play
In summer twilights long ago
Beneath the sun's last afterglow.

He was a gentle, merry lad
Friendly, and easily made glad.
But now the change! The marks of sin
Were graven deep, without, within.

His body, once so slender, trim
Was huge and gross. I looked at him
And wondered when and how and why
It came to pass; why he, not I?

I loved his mother, long since dead;
And so, thinking of her, I said

Just what she often used to say,
"Jimmy, have you been good today?"

"Not very, I'm afraid," he said
And hastily he turned his head.
I think he had not cried for years,
But now his eyes were filled with tears.

And suddenly I seemed to see
The little boy who used to be,
The small clean lad of yesterday
Who somehow, somewhere, missed the way.

He was bewildered, lost and sad,
He had not meant to be so bad.
It somehow "happened" . . . Then I tried
To tell him of the One who died,

Who took on Him the sins of men,
To make them pure and clean again.
He listened well to what I told
But he was hardened in the mold.

The twig was bent, the tree inclined,
And so his heart and soul and mind
Found it too hard a thing to do . . .
I thought of other young lads who

Are living in the plastic years.
Will they too know remorse and tears?
I lifted up my heart in prayer
For little children everywhere.

The tender lambs, still white and small.
I heard the loving Savior call,
"Bring them to Me, Forbid them not.
Feed thou my lambs-hast thou forgot?"

By Martha Snell Nicholson
Used by permission of Moody Press

Have we forgotten? We live in what is called a Christian nation, yet according to statistics an estimated 39 million of our children in America alone aren't receiving any Bible teaching at all!

I believe a special effort is needed to reach the children, and almost every one of you is in a position to reach some. I haven't found any place in my Bible where it says it is okay to go to our comfortable churches and sit every Sunday and wait for them to come in.

The Bible says, ". . . Go out into the highways and hedges, and compel them to come in . . ." (Luke 14:23 KJV). If that doesn't condone a bus route to bring them in, then I can't imagine what would. I praise God for every church that has realized this and started a bus route to bring in the children.

There are many ways to reach children for Christ. Junior Church (children's church) is a way I have seen work tremendously well. Vacation Bible School, camps, special parties and rallies, meetings, videos, and of course, Sunday school and church are other methods which work.

However, if you get the children into your church, whether it's by bus or individually, I hope you will make sure every one of your people who work with them know how to lead a child to Christ. I trust you will make sure they are receiving a simple "how to" message of salvation and an invitation to accept Christ. Don't ever let it be said about your church, "I attended there for 13 years and didn't know how to receive Jesus into my life."

Another way to reach children is by personal contact work. When you visit, do you look right past a child for an adult to reach? A good form of personal contact is open air work. This is taking an instrument (wordless book, gospel nut, hand, or some other such tool to get their attention) and going out to where the children are. Good places to find children are fairs, parks, streets, playgrounds, etc. (Check the laws in your city to make sure this is legal.) Give them the message of salvation and an invitation to receive Christ as their own personal Savior.

If you sent a missionary from your church over to some foreign country, you wouldn't expect them to build a church and then sit and wait for the people to come, would you? You would insist that they be out where the people are, reaching them for Christ and then bringing them into the church. Surely we need this in our nation today.

You can also reach the children God puts you personally in contact with such as friends, neighbors, and relatives. If you don't know any children, then ask God to put you in touch with some.

Another way to reach children, of which I have heard tremendous testimonies, is a telephone ministry, such as Dial-a-Story. I understand a young mother, or anyone who is unable to go out of their home, can reach out to hundreds, or perhaps in larger communities even thousands, through a telephone ministry.

The media (television, VCRs, DVDs, radio, newspaper) is another way we should be using to reach children with the message of salvation and an invitation to receive Christ. If we don't use these tools, the devil certainly will. In fact, he already is.

One of the methods to reach children for Christ which I am most excited about is Home Bible Clubs. I was completely unqualified to teach the Good News Clubs in Independence, but God said do it and I did. Because of mere obedience I had the opportunity to give the message of salvation and an invitation to receive Christ to over 300 different children in a few short years, and that's with a husband and five children of my own.

Many did receive Christ as their Savior, and a large number of them continued on with baptism and joined a church. Whole families were reached through these clubs. *Good News Clubs work!!*

Have you ever noticed what those excited Christians over in Acts were doing? They were teaching in the homes. Look it up. It's found in Acts 5-the last verse. We owe it to our nation, and we owe it to our children, most of all we owe it to our Savior to find and use every means God gives us to reach out to the lost in these last days; keeping in mind always, all these methods, all these means, are nothing more than going out and picking up the fruit that has already been won through intercessory prayer.

The greatest statement I can think of to close this book with is, "I waited patiently for the Lord, and He inclined unto me, and heard my cry. He brought me up also out of a horrible pit, out of the miry clay, and set my feet upon a rock, and established my goings. And He hath put a new song in my mouth, even praise unto our God: many shall see it and fear and shall trust the Lord" (Psalm 40:1-3 KJV).

God be with you.

For help in reaching children for Christ, contact:

Child Evangelism Fellowship
@International Headquarters
P.O. Box 348
Warrenton, MO. 63386-0348
Phone: 636-456-4321
www.cefonline